Algrove Publishing Limited
1090 Morrison Drive
Ottawa, Ontario
Canada K2H 1C2

National Library of Canada Cataloguing in Publication Data

Rockwell, F. F. (Frederick Frye), b. 1884
        Gardening with peat moss

Reprint of ed. originally published : New York : Atkins & Durbrow, 1928.
ISBN 1-894572-56-4

        1. Peat mosses. 2. Soil conditioners. 3. Peat as plant-growing
medium. 4. Gardening. I. Title. II. Series: Classic reprint series
(Ottawa, Ont.)

S661.2.P4R62 2002   635.9'1826   C2002-902625-3

Printed in Canada
#10602

Publisher's Note

The genesis of this little gardening book can be found in the automobile industry. Cars had become so popular by the mid-1920s and horses so much less popular that manure, the gardener's friend, was in short supply. As people looked for substitutes, peat moss rose in popularity, resulting in this small volume, which assures the reader that peat moss is actually superior to its predecessor.

Leonard G. Lee
Ottawa
March, 2002

GARDENING
WITH PEAT MOSS

A garden is a lovesome thing, God wot!
Rose plot,
Fringed pool,
Ferned grot . . . . . .

. . . . . . and yet the fool
Contends that God is not —
Not God! in gardens! when the eve is cool?
Nay, but I have a sign;
'Tis very sure God walks in mine.

—BROWN

GARDENING
WITH
PEAT MOSS

A GUIDE TO EASIER METHODS IN GROWING MORE
BEAUTIFUL FLOWERS, SHRUBS AND TREES AND
MAKING MORE PERMANENT LAWNS

BY

F. F. ROCKWELL

Author of Around The Year In The Garden;
The Book of Bulbs; Gardening Under Glass;
The Home Garden Handbooks, etc.

AND

WM. G. BREITENBUCHER

Published by

ATKINS & DURBROW, INC.

29 Burling Slip, New York

Distributors of Garden Peat Moss

Printed in the United States
by The Du Bois Press, Rochester, N.Y.

FOREWORD

The Reason For This Volume

This is not "just another book about gardening;" nor is it merely a piece of publicity for peat moss.

Gardening with peat moss is a subject which will interest thousands, very many thousands, of persons in this country because *gardening with manure is no longer possible*—for the simple reason that manure is not available and peat moss is the best thing to use in its place.

You may notice that I did not say "the best substitute for manure." Peat moss is incomparably more than a substitute for manure. In horticultural use it will produce many of the results possible with manure; but it does so many other things that it is in a class by itself. If I had to garden without manure or without peat moss I would by all odds select the peat moss. Three years ago I would have decided the other way.

Before undertaking to cooperate in the writing of this book, I conducted a series of practical experiments, in my own garden. They were not "laboratory" experiments, and not what scientists would call scientific experiments: there was plenty of data of this sort available. What I desired was to satisfy myself that peat moss was the great discovery *for the amateur gardner, in everyday practical work,* which it seemed to be, and which my own use and observation of it indicated. The results of scientific experiments were to me of secondary conconcern: I have been familiar with too many things which gave marvelous results on an experimental basis, but which failed to work out in practice.

The results of my own use of peat moss, in practical work, have been in many directions so astonishing that I would have found it difficult to have believed them if I had not actually done the work with my own hands, as well as seen the effect with my own eyes. Even so I would have hesitated to recount the results of some of this work, solely on the basis of my own experience, if I had not found, upon personal investigation, that they checked up with carefully conducted, really scientific experiments, by wholly disinterested institutions.

Therefore I feel that in the subject of "Gardening with Peat Moss" there is a real and important message for the amateur gardener, which will make his way easier and his achievements more certain. I believe that in helping to call this fact to the attention of those who are about to begin gardening, or who, having gardens, aspire to still more successful ones. I shall be doing them a genuinely helpful turn.

In the preparation of this book I have enjoyed the privilege of the close cooperation of my friend Mr. Wm. G. Breitenbucher. Without his part in it, it would have fallen far short of whatever merit it may now possess. I do not know of any other man in this country who has so complete a knowledge of both the practical and the theoretical sides of the horticultural uses and properties of peat moss as that possessed by Mr. Breitenbucher. He has devoted many years to a close study of this subject in gardens, in greenhouses, and in laboratories in this country, and followed the work of the German scientists who, so far, have dug further into peats and moss peats than anyone else.

To the readers of this volume, therefore, I can promise a subject full of interest, full of information, and full, I believe, of time-saving and profit-making or pleasure-yielding suggestions. I will go so far as to say I believe it would not be too strong a statement to claim that the intelligent use of peat moss is going to revolutionize many phases of gardening for the amateur. "Revolutionize" is defined: "To cause an entire change in the character of."

Regarding the above statement, you may be inclined either to smile or to scoff. Do either, but don't neglect to look further into the subject; and don't formulate your opinions about peat moss until you have actually tried it out in your garden.

CONTENTS

CHAP. I WHAT PEAT MOSS IS, AND WHAT IT BRINGS TO THE GARDEN.

My first experience with peat moss as a garden material; a real discovery; what peat moss is and how it is obtained; why it is a boon to the home gardener; what it accomplishes in the garden.

CHAP. II HOW PLANTS GROW: THE ALL-IMPORTANT FUNCTION OF MOISTURE.

A little study of plant growth; some general rules as to plant nutrition; the secret of the astonishing results secured with peat moss.

CHAP. III PLANTS FROM SEEDS AND CUTTINGS.

Every true gardener must know at least the a-b-c of plant propagation—the making of new plants; growing plants from seed; the fascinating work of growing plants from cuttings; moisture constancy an important factor.

CHAP. IV PLANTING AND TRANSPLANTING.

Success with plants in the garden and about the grounds depends largely upon successful planting and transplanting; the one great cause of failure in this work, and how to overcome it; better results with transplanting than you have ever before succeeded in getting.

CHAP. V   LAWNS—THEIR MAKING, RE-MAKING, AND KEEPING.

The lawn will make or mar the beauty of the place; lawn grasses, and why it is difficult to get a perfect turf; building a lawn for beauty *and* permancy; repairing and renovating lawns; care of the lawn, soil humus vs. constant watering.

CHAP. VI   SUCCESS WITH ROSES.

The amazing mortality among garden roses; its chief cause; the three vital uses of peat moss in rose growing—in the soil; as a winter mulch; as a summer mulch.

CHAP. VII   EVERGREENS AND EVERGREEN SHRUBS.

Coniferous evergreens—among the most permanent of all trees and the most difficult to start successfully; why they are difficult to establish, the cause of "second year" deaths, and how to remedy it: Rhododendrons, most azaleas, laurel and other acid-loving plants; how peat moss takes the kinks out of their successful culture.

CHAP. VIII   MAKING SURE OF RESULTS WITH LILIES AND BULBS.

The peculiar and quite different requirements of these two classes of plants; the most general causes of failure with each; how peat moss works to secure success with both.

CHAP. IX   HARDY PERENNIALS AND ROCK PLANTS.

Why the hardy perennial border peters out; how to overcome the handicap of artificial conditions in growing them; making a new perennial border; remaking an old one; peat moss as a manure substitute; and as an ideal mulch.

CHAP. X   PLANTS IN THE HOUSE.

Why so few plants succeed in the house; why grandmother had better "luck" with house plants than we do; the return of the old-fashioned indoor garden; success depends chiefly upon maintaining even soil moisture; peat moss essential in building an ideal soil; growing bulbs in peat moss; success with ferns indoors.

Gardening with Peat Moss

CHAPTER I

WHAT PEAT MOSS IS AND WHAT IT BRINGS TO THE GARDEN

Perhaps you have never heard of peat moss. Or possibly, even if you have, the word does not mean anything very clear and definite to you. In this little book, we are going to talk about gardening with peat moss, and so, naturally, the reader will want to know, first of all, just what peat moss is.

Peat Moss is a particular kind of peat. It might have been more correctly called "moss peat" rather than peat moss; because it is the type of peat which was formed from various mosses. "Peat" has been called by someone "Coal that never got hard." That is a suggestive definition, because peat, like coal, was originally, growing plants or vegetable matter which in the course of time became covered over, and remained buried, for centuries, beneath succeeding layers of plant growth. Concerning the various kinds of peat, and their difference in texture and composition more will be said later.

Peat is found in all countries. It occurs in swamps or bogs which may have formed pockets creating just the right conditions to make peat out of the decaying vegetable matter which they contain. The peat itself might be termed "decayed vegetable matter," or "humus," in a state of *arrested* decay— packed away where it would be preserved in perfect condition for ages. Almost may one conceive of old Mother Nature saying to herself "It seems a shame to waste all this beautiful rich compost! I will lock it up here safely for a few aeons, and some day my helpers, who seek to assist me in clothing the earth with beauty, will find it and use it to grow finer plants and flowers!"

And, centuries later, men did discover these treasure stores of peat, and have utilized it for many purposes. In some places, such as Holland, long famous for its wonderful production in horticulture and agriculture—it is cultivated where it lies, or used locally to improve poorer soil. In Ireland, the peat bogs furnish much of the nation's fuel supply. In Germany, it has been utilized not only for farming and horticultural purposes, but as bedding material for animals, as insulating material in the building of store houses and dwelling houses, and for packing all kinds of fruits and vegetables for preserving and for long distance shipment.

My first acquaintance with peat moss, as a youngster, was when a neighbor of ours who kept a very fine driving stable, and who bought large quantities of rye straw from us for bedding, began using this "new-fangled" material instead. As a result, he had use for much less straw—so naturally, I was not very favorably impressed with the peat moss! But further investigation showed that his stables were always clean, sweet and *dry,* as the result of the wonderful power which this material seemed to have of soaking up and holding all liquids within reach. And so we ourselves began using it for bedding. But this peat moss, while it was excellent for this purpose, disintigrated in the soil very slowly; lumps of it would seem to stick about for years before going to pieces. As a result we used it on the farm crops, such as corn, grain, potatoes and hay, but kept it off the vegetable garden and onion field. Many years later, when I first began to notice peat moss being advocated for garden use, I recalled this former experience and was very skeptical concerning it. To me peat moss was just plain peat moss. I knew nothing concerning the different types or different grades. That prejudice, accidently acquired, kept me from trying it, even in an experimental way, for many years. I was indeed fortunate to discover as soon as I did that some particular types of peat moss, properly prepared, are perfectly adapted to garden use.

What Peat Moss Brings to the Home Garden

What first really interested me in the horticultural possibilities of peat moss were the remarkable results achieved with it, both in propagation and in growing, at the nurseries of Koster and Company at Bridgeton. I was, at that time, a director in this concern, and living within a mile of it, and as much of the work was entirely new to me—involving as it

2

Peat moss from the first and second layers in a peat bog. That at left showing fine, even texture, is suitable for horticultural purposes; the other, coarse, and containing roots and foreign matter, is not.

(Above) Quality Garden Peat Moss is always packed in bales.
(Below) A sea-side garden planned and planted by the author at Cape May,
New Jersey. Peat moss made possible the results obtained (see text).

did the production of plants which had been formerly grown almost exclusively in Holland—I was tremendously interested in seeing how things were done.

I soon discovered that peat moss was the backbone of all the propagating operations, and a most important factor in the continued successful growing of the plants after they had reached the fields. The former was a surprise to me, for, while I knew that peat moss was sometimes employed as a propagating material, I had always used sand when I had greenhouses of my own, and knew from familiarity with many commercial establishments, and with current literature on propagating, that sand was considered the standard medium for rooting cuttings. I was surprised also to see that the peat moss was used out of doors, not only as a material for mulching, but also in soil building and plant growing generally. Seeing these remarkable results, I began to use peat moss myself for many different garden purposes, and these experiments were extended when the possibility of the preparation of the present book was considered.

It is not theory, therefore, but the outgrowth of several years personal practical experience and observation, which convinces me that peat moss is one of the greatest helps ever presented to the home gardener. It offers him aid for more different purposes, and to a higher degree of perfection, than any other material of which I know.

As a substitute for manure, peat moss may be employed with confidence in the results it will produce. Ordinary commercial fertilizers fail to serve as a manure substitute for the simple reason that a great deal of the value of manure is due to the moisture holding humus which it contains, as well as to the comparatively small amounts of actual plant food. (All this is explained in more detail in the following chapter.) Manure has become increasingly hard to get. The farmer has found a satisfactory substitute in "green manures"—crops grown and plowed under green for the purpose of enriching the soil. This substitute, however, is not available to the home gardener except to a very limited extent, and not at all for the flower garden or the lawn.

As a soil improver, that is, as a material to improve the *mechanical* condition of the soil, peat moss has no superior. It helps to bind together and to give more body to loose, sandy soil, and to break up and render more friable heavy and clay soils.

As a propagating medium, both for starting seeds and rooting cuttings, peat moss is unquestionably without an equal. It supplies to perfection the requisite mechanical conditions—moisture holding capacity, drainage, and aeration—to assure the highest possible results in the germination of seed, and the formation of new roots from cuttings. But more than this, due to its peculiar—and as yet unexplained—stimulation of root development, it is in a class by itself.

As a forcing medium, for the growing of bulbs in bowls, or plants in pans or pots, it has proved superior to everything else which has been tried. (In chapter 10, you will find more information on this point.)

As a mulch, peat moss meets every requirement. Being an excellent insulating material, it keeps out heat and cold; it does not pack down; it allows the air to penetrate; it is light; and it may be easily either removed or worked lightly into the soil.

As a storing material, for keeping such roots as dahlias, cannas, or tuberous begonias, which are sometimes difficult to handle, fleshy roots like bleeding heart, and the roots of dormant plants such as roses, which may have to be held temporarily awaiting planting, it is both convenient and astonishingly efficaceous. It may, in fact, be used to great advantage for the storing of vegetables and fruits, as well as flower bulbs. Toma-

Apples of the same variety kept for the same length of time in the ordinary way, and packed in peat moss. Due to its ideal insulating qualities, peat moss preserves the natural moisture in roots, bulbs, or fruits, which are packed in it.

4

toes packed in peat moss will keep for months. (One of the accompanying cuts shows results with apples.) Here is a use for this excellent material which we cannot dwell upon here, but which may well be followed up by anyone keeping fruits and vegetables through the winter.

Availability and convenience. And finally, this remarkable gardener's assistant is always ready for use. It keeps indefinitely; may be stored anywhere, even outdoors in the open; is clean, convenient to use, and absolutely sterile. Contrary to other fertilizers and manures, it actually invites your use. You like to bury your fingers in the clean, brown flaky particles— it does not soil nor stain the hands; merely brush the palms together and they are again clean.

Show me any other one material available for garden use which will do for the gardener one-half the things which peat moss does and I will admit that I am too enthusiastic about peat moss—but not until then!

CHAPTER II

HOW PLANTS GROW

THE ALL IMPORTANT FUNCTION OF MOISTURE

No gardener is so good a gardener as he may be until he has learned something of *how* plants grow. And when he stops to take a peek into this fascinating subject, he will find it one of the most vividly interesting things he ever investigated. Not only will it make of him a better gardener, but it will open up to him an entirely new world for observation, and give him a keener and richer appreciation of all plants.

It would take a volume many times the size of this to discuss the subject of plant growth in a comprehensive way. All that may be attempted here is to sketch it briefly in the simplest of terms; but even such an inadequate presentation will help to some extent in explaining how plants grow, and why peat moss produces the seemingly wonderful results it does.

EACH PLANT A LIVING, BREATHING, INDIVIDUAL ORGANISM

Perhaps the first thing to be realized is that every plant, from the tiniest seedling in your coldframe to the most stalwart ancient oak upon the hill, is an individual organism.

Like any animal, it is a complex structure, composed of groups of living cells, or "protoplasm." As in animal life, these cells form tissues and organs, each having a special duty to perform in carrying on the growth of the plant, and in helping to accomplish its purpose in the scheme of things. How these tissues and organs function, and their relation and reaction to soil and atmospheric conditions, constitutes the fascinating story of plant growth. It is only when we know something of this story that we can comprehend why plants grow well under some conditions, and under others fail to do so.

Plants are like animals in many respects; they must have food and drink, they react to heat and cold. Their ultimate aim, so far as nature is concerned, is to reproduce themselves. To this purpose they are, for the most part, supplied with sex

6

organs. The beauty of the rose, the fragrance of migonette, were not primarily for the delectation of man, but a means of attracting insects to carry the life transmitting pollen from one plant to another. Plants, like animals, prosper and thrive under good care and favorable conditions, and languish and perish where conditions are not favorable.

But plants are unlike animals in two very important respects.

In the first place, they cannot go in search of their food; food must be found, or be placed, within their reach.

And secondly, they can take their foods only *in solution.* They live on soup, and very, very weak soup at that; soup so attenuated, that the proverbial restaurant clam broth would seem a rich stew by comparison!

Moisture Absolutely Essential to Plant Growth

It is this last fact which gives us the actual key to plant nutrition. Plants themselves are made up of from 60 to 95% of clear water: the great majority of them much nearer the latter figure than the former. But that is not all. For every pound of water which remains and actually becomes part of the plant, 95 to 99 pounds are lost through evaporation, or "transpired" through the leaves. In other words, for each pound of dry matter, or actual solids, in every plant in your garden, there has been taken from the soil from 550 to 950 pounds of water —($\frac{1}{4}$ to $\frac{1}{2}$ a ton).

Read that over again, and let it soak in, then you will begin to understand what an important part water plays in plant growth. The luxuriance of the tropical jungle is due not so much to high temperature, as to the inexhaustible supply of moisture. The deserts are hotter than the jungles, but water is lacking.

How Plants Eat, and Drink. The poet, in his intuitive way, often stumbles directly upon the fact which the scientist, with his microscope and test tubes, has been searching the world to find. When Joyce Kilmer, in his much quoted poem "Trees" penned the lines:—

> "A tree whose hungry roots are pressed
> Against the earth's sweet flowing breast."

he put the whole thing in a couplet.

7

The mouth of a plant is made up of innumerable fiberous "feeding" roots which are developed along the larger main roots, usually more generously towards the ends of the newer main roots, as they gradually die off along the older portions, much as a tree loses its lower branches. The soil moisture, containing extremely weak solutions of the various plant foods is absorbed through the root hairs which cover the feeding roots, and are in reality minute porous hollow tubes. Once within the roots, the solutions begin to undergo chemical changes and are converted into what the layman knows as the "sap" of the plant, which is carried upward by a force called "osmosis" through branches and stems to the leaves.

How the Plant Foods Are Used. Once the diluted food elements are absorbed through the root hair membranes they remain within the plant. Sometimes the roots excrete traces of chemical elements which they cannot utilize as food, but the root excretions consist almost entirely of carbon-dioxide; this is the result of the breathing or respiration of the root cells, which in this respect function like the cells of the stems and leaves. Within the plant, oxygen and hydrogen are combined to form certain starches and sugars, which are known as "carbohydrates." This process can take place only in the presence of light, and in those cells of the plant which contain chlorophyll —the substance which gives the green color to plants.

From the carbo-hydrates and certain mineral elements such as potassium, phosphorus, and sulphur, there are formed more complex compounds—the proteins, and organic acids. These last three elements, together with nitrogen, are utlized in the formation of new cells, so that the growth of the plant depends upon their being present in the soil in sufficient quantities.

But here is the thing to keep in mind. No matter how plentiful they may be, *the plant roots cannot take them up unless there is also sufficient moisture in the soil to hold them in solution.* Not one of these materials can enter the plant, even in the minutest quantity, unless it is carried in in this solution. Water not only brings the food into the plant, but transports it from one part of the plant to another.

And thus the process of plant growth goes on. The raw materials, in solution, are absorbed through the root tissues; are changed and combined, largely by the action of sunlight,

There is an intimate relation between the character of the soil and the development of root growth. Plants can absorb food only through the root hairs on the fine feeding roots. Peat moss stimulates root development.

The plants at the left of the watering can are of the same variety, planted ten days earlier, in the same type of soil, as the plants at the extreme left in the right hand photograph. Notice height of plants of this and of other varieties, in proportion to the stakes, which are all six feet. The plants in the right hand photograph received an application of one bale of peat moss to a bed 6 x 30 feet. Needless to say, this grower now uses peat moss for all his dahlias.

into forms which the plant can "digest"; and then re-distributed, through the flow of sap, to produce new cells, which in turn form new buds, leaves, flowers, and fruits, and also push out still further the spreading root system, which searches out fresh sources of food. Plant roots, incidentally, have a most uncanny capacity for locating and heading straight for any new resevoirs of moisture or of plant food which may be within reach. Make a note of this last fact, because it is important and we will have occasion to refer to it again.

Plant Foods

By analyzing plants in the laboratory, scientists are able to determine exactly of what "elements" they are composed. Such analysis have revealed the fact that there are ten essential elements which must be present at all times to make normal growth possible.

Of these ten essential elements, carbon comes from the carbon-dioxide of the air; oxygen from the air and from the soil water; and hydrogen from the water which is present at all times in any living plant.

Of the remaining seven elements, nitrogen, potassium and phosphorus are the most important. These it is usually necessary to add to the soil by applying fertilizer or manure. In the "analysis" printed on a bag of commercial fertilizer, you will find them given as Ammonia, Phosphoric Acid, and Potash. The other four, calcium, magnesium, iron and sulphur, are present in sufficient quantities in most soils.

All plants utilize these various food elements, but different kinds of plants use them in different proportions. The plant is capable of making its own selection. But here is an interesting—and a most important—fact: if there is a shortage of any one element, no surplus of the others can make up for it. This is often the cause of unsatisfactory growth under conditions which may seem ideal. It is impossible to get plants to make a satisfactory growth on a one-sided or a lop-sided diet while it is true that "the soil must be rich or the garden will be poor," it is also true that the richness must be suitably balanced.

Effects of Different Fertilizers. The results which the three most important chemical elements—nitrogen, phosphoric acid and potash—have upon plant growth, are quite different. If one is familiar with these differences, it is often possible to determine, even without a soil analysis, the kind of plant food likely to be lacking where growth is not satisfactory.

Nitrogen is most important in stimulating and developing new growth, and especially foliage growth. Lack of nitrogen is usually quickly noticable in a slowing down or a checking of the growth, and in a pale or yellowish caste of foliage. An excess of nitrogen often produces a too rapid and soft, flabby growth, which is undesirable at any time, and particularly so late in the season, as it is abnormally tender and subject to winter injuries of various kinds.

Phosphoric acid is essential to vigorous and firm growth, especially of the woody parts of the plant, flower stems, and so forth. Also it seems to affect to some extent the degree of color or pigmentation. Too much phosphoric acid checks foliage growth, and hastens the formation of flowers and fruits.

Potash is required by most plants in more generous amounts as they reach maturity, either of the entire plant, or of a crop of fruits or seed.

An ordinary high-grade, "balanced" fertilizer contains 4 to 6% of nitrogen, 5 to 8% of phosphoric acid, and 4 to 10% of potash. The commercial grower, using large quantities of fertilizer, makes a careful study of the exact fertilizer requirements of each individual crop. For the home gardener, growing a number of different things, this is not practicable. His aim should be, plenty of each of the three elements required without a proportionate excess of any.

"Available Plant Food." In garden literature, particularly in discussions concerning fertilizer, you will come across the term "available plant food."

What Is "Available Plant Food?" In a word, it means merely food that is available for the plant's use. We have already seen that plants can obtain no food excepting that which is held in solution in the soil moisture. Available plant foods, therefore, are those which are *soluble in soil moisture.* No others are available. And until they are, plants may actually starve in a soil which is stocked full of plant food—just as might a child locked up in a warehouse full of canned goods in cases.

Much of the plant food which the soil naturally contains, and much of that which is added to it in the form of fertilizer, gradually becomes available through the process of decomposition. This process is greatly hastened by the presence in the soil of various beneficial bacteria. These bacteria, however, can themselves thrive and multiply only in soil which contains a certain percentage of moisture. If it is too dry or too wet, they immediately perish by the billions, and as a result the work of decomposition, which is releasing plant foods locked up in the soil, is checked. So it is evident that indirectly, as well as directly, abundant moisture in the soil is essential to vigorous plant growth.

"Acid" and "Sweet" Soils. The bacteria which are favorable to most forms of plant growth cannot live in soil which is too acid in its reaction. Lime is, therefore, frequently used to "sweeten" such soils. This element has the property of combining with certain toxic substances in the soil, locking them up in the form of insoluble compounds, and at the same time, releasing useful elements which were before unavailable. Thus, while lime is not directly a plant food, under many conditions it helps tremendously in forwarding plant growth.

Some plants, however, such as rhododendrons, laurel, azaleas and heath, or erica, differ directly from the majority in that they require an acid reacting soil, and will not grow in a sweet soil no matter how rich it may be. These plants are, as a general group, termed "ericaceous" plants; for them, lime is not only not beneficial, but directly and often fatally injurious.

Why Peat Moss is the Ideal Moisture Holder

From even a glance at the foregoing outline of the process of plant growth, it is overwhelmingly evident that the supply of moisture in the soil is an all important factor in the control of plant growth. This being so, the next question is how best to control the supply of moisture in the soil.

Water, of course, is being constantly removed from the soil. Before an hour is up, following a rain, or after we have applied water artificially, it begins to go. The surplus runs off the surface, or passes down into the subsoil as drainage; and water is lost from the surface of the soil through constant evaporation. The plants themselves, as we have seen, take up and evaporate through their leaves enormous quantities of water in the process of growth. How, then, is the water supply to be maintained?

The value of manure, sometimes considered indispensible for gardening purposes, is due in large part to its capacity for absorbing and holding moisture in the humus matter which it contains. It also supplies nitrogen in an immediately available form, and this provides a quick stimulation to plant growth, which is obvious to any observer.

In granulated peat moss, however, we have a material which is capable of absorbing and holding many times more water than the best of manure. Some idea as to the tremendous absorption power of peat moss may be had from the following figures, the result of a recent careful test made by one of the leading scientific institutions of the country. These tests showed that peat moss would absorb and hold seven times its own dry weight—that is 700% of water—when wet to the saturation point.

In contrast to this, good garden loam showed itself capable of holding about one half of its own dry weight, or to be exact, 55%; while sand absorbed about one-fifth of its own weight, or 22%. The accompanying diagram presents these figures in graphic form. You know how quickly sand will dry

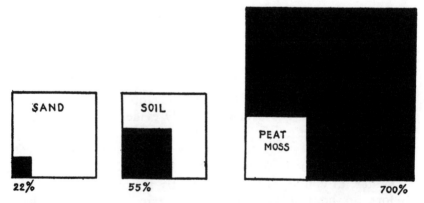

Why peat moss makes plants grow. The three cubes above represent by weight equal quantities of sand, good garden loam, and granulated peat moss. The *black* portions represent the amount of moisture absorbed by each: 22% for sand, 55% for the garden loam, and 700% for the peat moss.

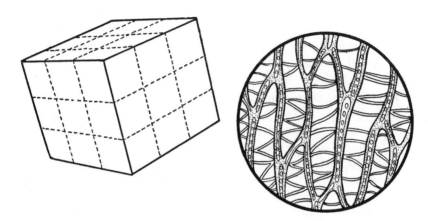

(*Right*) Interior construction of the water cell of sphagnum moss peat, magnified many times (after A. J. Werth, from Torfstreu and Torfmull-Rahm).

Peat moss not only absorbs and holds moisture itself, but by keeping the soil in a loose, finely pulverized condition enables it also to retain more moisture, through increasing the surface area of the soil particles. A glance at the diagram above illustrates this. The large single cube has a surface area of 27 cubic inches, whereas, when broken up into 27 smaller cubes, the surface area is increased to 162 square inches.

out, compared to good garden soil; and yet the difference between the absorption qualities of these two materials is not nearly so great as the difference between good garden loam and peat moss! This will give you some idea of the tremendous water holding capacity of the latter material.

How Peat Moss Holds So Much Water. High grade horticultural peat moss is mined from bogs of sphagnum peat, that is, peat which was originally, centuries ago, sphagnum moss. Sphagnum moss is among the oldest plants which survive to the present day. Almost everyone is familiar with fresh sphagnum moss. It may be found growing in most swampy sections, and is used almost universally by nurserymen and florists for packing around the roots of plants, and for other purposes where it is desired to hold moisture for a long period. The cell structure of sphagnum moss is decidedly different from that of most plants. Under the microscope, the cells of sphagnum are like a series of empty rooms, with spiral or spring-like supporting filiments which serve merely as a reinforcement to prevent the delicate walls from collapsing.

13

The rooms themselves are flooded with water. It is this tremendous interior surface in the cell structure of the plant, unlike that of any other vegetable organism, which gives it its great capacity for holding water. (The diagram on page 13 shows the formation of the cell structure.)

To manufacture the best grade of horticultural or garden peat moss, the highest grade sphagnum moss peat is dug from the bog in the form of huge bricks. These are packed mountain high in such a manner that the air can circulate freely through them. Even so, its takes a year and a half or more for the peat to dry out sufficiently to be handled, ground up and pulverized, and packed and shipped, in the form of granulated peat moss. This product is, of course, quite different from that obtained from peat resulting from materials *other* than sphagnum moss, such as wood-peat, cane-peat and inferior grades of sphagnum peat which have foreign materials mixed through them.

Often the inexperienced planter makes the mistake of using some other type of peat, or a coarse grade of moss-peat, which is suitable only for stable or for farm purposes, and is not adapted to garden use. The results, naturally, are not as satisfactory as when granulated, high grade moss-peat is employed.

Peat Moss Assures Moisture Constancy. Recent scientific experiments tend to prove that the constancy of the water supply in the soil, as well as the total amount, is an important factor in plant growth. This, of course, merely substantiates a belief which practical growers have long held. It is only one of the reasons why irrigation produces bigger crops even in climates where the total rainfall should be sufficient to supply the maximum growth. Peat moss not only absorbs moisture, but holds on to it tenaceously.

Peat Moss holds the moisture just where it is needed. The German authority, Dr. G. Kowallik compares granulated peat moss to "billions and billions of tiny sponges." I doubt if a better description could be found. These myriads of minute sponges mixed through the soil, hold the life-giving water directly where the thirsty plant roots can most conveniently find it and make use of it.

A "block" of rhododendrons grown at the nurseries of Koster & Co. Peat moss is used freely from the starting of the seedlings, to the setting out of the grafted plants in the field. The insert shows a rhododendron plant from Le Bar's Rhododendron Nurseries, and the root development secured by the generous use of peat moss.

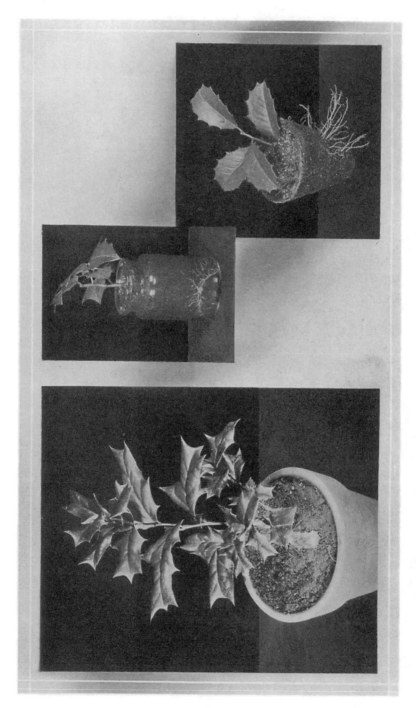

Holly, long considered difficult to propagate by cuttings, roots readily in peat moss. In the glass jar you can see the root development after several weeks growth. A new type of pot, made of peat moss, permits the plant roots to grow directly into the walls of the pot—pot and all being transplanted.

CHAPTER III

PLANTS FROM SEEDS AND CUTTINGS

Propagation is the art, or science—for it partakes of both—
by which the gardener obtains additional plants from seed or
cuttings. Anyone who grows plants at all, from a pot or two
of geraniums on the window sill, to the beds and borders of
a large estate, will sooner or later want to try his or her hand
at this most fascinating phase of gardening.

The commonest method of producing new plants is, of
course, from seed; but not all plants come "true" from seed,
and therefore, it is often desirable to obtain the new plants
from cuttings or "slips" of the parent plant. All the genuine
Koster Blue Spruces are descendants of a single individual blue
spruce tree which happened to be more beautiful than the
several thousand other little blue spruces which were grown
from the same lot of seed. Cuttings and grafts from this tree,
painstakingly nursed under the skillful hands of the Hollander
who discovered it, gave more of exactly the same kind; and
from these, in turn, were produced others, until he and his
neighbor nurserymen, had sufficient to ship to every clime
where spruces may be grown.

There are numerous other methods of propagating employed
by the nurseryman and florist, such as budding, grafting, root-
grafting, and layering. But the two of chief interest to the
amateur, are growing from seeds and from cuttings. Once
he has gained mastery over these two methods, he need never
want for additional plants to further beautify his own grounds
or to have a surplus to give away or to "swap" with his
neighbors.

PLANTS FROM SEED

Most persons who have attempted any gardening at all,
have grown some plants from seed. A number of the annual
flowers, and a few of the perennials, grow so readily that it
is almost impossible to fail with them. A child could plant
sunflowers or coreopsis and succeed with them. Many amateurs
achieve fair results with the larger or more easily grown flower

15

seeds, but each year there are thousands upon thousands of failures, and consequent disappointment and discouragement, with flower seed which *should* have germinated satisfactorily and brought beauty and joy to countless garden lovers.

And the sad part of it is that most of these failures were wholly unnecessary. With a little experience, and a reasonable amount of care, even the amateur can get almost any seed to germinate satisfactorily, provided they are alive and sound. Would you not like to grow from seed not only the easy things, but any of the fine new perennials you wish for your hardy border? And wouldn't you like to feel, even with the annuals and the ordinary, easily grown perenials, that success is a certainty instead of hoping and waiting in uncertainty with each lot of seed, and possibly failing after all, as too often happens?

How Seeds Work. A seed, when you stop to consider it, is really a marvelous piece of mechanism. Here, within a bomb-like shell—so tiny that in some instances, you almost need a microscope to see it—lies hidden the infinitesimal germ of life which may have to lie dormant for weeks, months, or even years, before it receives the signal from outside automatically to set itself off! Compared with such a masterpiece as this, how crude seems the cleverest bomb ever contrived by human ingenuity!

The stimulus required to bring this apparently dead thing, a dry seed, back to life, is the correct combination of moisture and temperature. Given this, the covering of the seed, usually tough, frequently extremely hard, but nevertheless very sensitive, responds. The life within, which has been arrested, miraculously starts anew. With a force which, if it could be measured in terms of pounds-pressure-per-square-inch, would be simply stupendous, the swelling germ bursts from its sealed coffin, and sends one tiny sprout upward towards the sunshine and the air, and another downward in search of moisture and food.

From then on, if conditions are favorable, growth is marvelously rapid. Every hour, almost, there is appreciable development. You go to bed one night, with no sign that anything is happening, and the next morning, tiny sprouts are pushing up through the surface—lifting and overthrowing what, in proportion to their own size, are huge slabs of soil weighing tons.

Truly, familiarity breeds contempt. All this miracle of seed germination and growth we take for granted. The real wonder is that seeds can thus resurrect themselves, come to life, and push their way out of the soil prison, even under the most favorable conditions. And yet we cover them with loads of soil they cannot possibly lift, with soil that bakes, under repeated waterings, to a cement-like crust, and dries out so thoroughly to the depth at which the seeds are planted, that the delicate first tendril-like root is shrivelled to a crisp—and then we write in to the seedsman and tell him that his seeds are no good!

The Proper Soil For Starting Seeds. A medium for the germination of seeds which would be theoretically ideal would score 100 percent on each of the five following points.

Retention of Moisture—to maintain a constant, even supply.

Porousness—to permit immediate draining off of any surplus water.

Friable Texture—which will not bake or "crust" on the surface.

Non-conductor of heat and cold—tending to maintain steady temperature despite fluctuations in atmospheric temperature.

Sterile—no disease germs lying to wait to attack the tiny and tender seedlings.

Let us see how granulated peat moss measures up on this exacting score card.

As to its moisture absorbing and holding quality, we have already explained somewhat in detail, why it leads all other materials. So far as drainage is concerned, it is simply impossible to make peat moss wet in the sense of being muddy. When the series of "tiny sponges" of which it consists, have absorbed water to their full capacity, any surplus immediately runs through and drains off. Too much water will never make them "run together" as happens with particles of finely sifted soil. For the same reason peat moss, wet or dry, never forms a crust. It will not wash over and bury the finest of seeds, such as those of tuberous-rooted begonias, which are sown directly on the surface; and any seeds which are covered can push up through it without meeting resistance. As to temperature changes, we have already seen that, due to its cellular construction, peat moss is a most effective non-conductor. Once the seed pans have been warmed up to the desired temprature, they will tend to retain it evenly, despite temporary fluctuations in the atmosphere. And finally, peat moss is absolutely sterile. "Mined" from beneath the earth's surface, where it has lain for centuries, it is so free from possible injurious bacteria that it is admitted as sterile even under the extremely stringent rules of the Federal Plant Quarantine. This is a most important fact, and accounts to no small degree for the success attained with it both in starting seeds and in rooting cuttings.

The Unknown "X" in Peat Moss Action

The above combination of qualities in granulated peat moss, would make it the best of all home materials for seed germination, even if it did not possess one remarkable additional characteristic which places it in a class entirely by itself.

Scientific investigators, both here and abroad, for many years have been puzzled by the remarkable stimulation of root-growth which peat moss produces, alike with seeds, cuttings, and growing plants. This is so marked, that certain of these investigators, such as Bottomley and his co-workers, have arrived at the conclusion that peat moss must contain some substances which they have not yet been able to isolate, which is responsible for this root development. These theoretical substances would seem most likely to be due to some special type of bacterial decomposition, and have been given the name of "auximones;" or, as they might be termed, auxiliary bacteriological helpers.

Details of Seed Propagation

Whether seeds are to be started under glass, in the house or greenhouse, in a coldframe or hotbed, or out-of-doors in the open, granulated peat moss will be found to render the work easier, more pleasant and much more certain.

For the majority of seeds, pure granulated peat moss is superior to a mixture or compost. It consists of decayed vegetable matter, which contains sufficient plant food to start the little seedlings off, and to continue vigorous growth until they are old enough to transplant. The advantages in using the pure peat moss are two: there is less danger of infection with injurious bacteria or disease spores, and the seedlings will make a more rapid growth, also lessening the danger of their being attacked by one of the several "damping off" diseases which often prove fatal. This is due in part to the fact that peat moss, as we have seen, retains an even moisture; whereas the alternate soaking and drying out of the soil, provides ideal conditions for many bacteria and fungi.

Granulated peat moss, which has been exposed to the air for months in its preparation, shows only a slightly acid reaction, and is not in the least injurious to the great majority of flower or vegetable seeds. For the lime-lovers, which are extremely sensitive to an acid condition, this acidity may readily be neutralized by adding a very small amount of lime, (¼ lb. to one cubic yard of peat), or a half-and-half mixture of light garden loam and peat will usually prove sufficiently "sweet."

Whether the peat is used alone, or in mixture with sand or soil, it is well to run the peat, or the mixture, through a small hand screen of about ¼" mesh, or preferably even finer, to get it absolutely fine and even. Moisten it thoroughly, turning it over several times in the process, *before* putting it in the flats or seed pans in which the seed is to be sown. Pack it down evenly, especially in the corners, leaving a half-inch or slightly less of space between the surface and the top edge of the box or pan.

Sowing The Seed. If the seed used is extremely fine, such as that of begonia, and many of the hardy perennials, it should be merely sown *on* the surface, and pressed in, without being covered at all. Larger seeds, such as pansies, may be covered a fraction of an inch, barely from sight; still larger ones a quarter of an inch or so. It is not necessary to water the top of the soil; if earth is being used, it may be fatal to do this; with peat moss, it is not so serious, but even in the latter case, it is much better to water thoroughly *before* the seed is sown, and then let the surface dry off before sowing. It is better still, to sow the seed and then place the vessel in a pan or tub of water, letting it soak up *from beneath* until the surface appears moist. This gives the most thorough saturation possible, without the slightest danger of disturbing the surface, and washing out and covering up some of the seed.

19

After sowing, place the seeds in a suitable temperature. This will be 55 to 65 degrees for the hardier flowers, such as pansies, sweet alysum, snapdragons and so forth, and 10 degrees higher for the more tender varieties such as salvia, begonias or heliotrope. For the first three or four days after sowing, these temperatures may be somewhat exceeded.

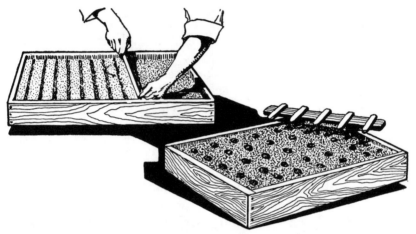

Seed box ready for sowing small seeds. They should be barely covered from sight; or, if very fine, merely pressed into the surface.

A convenient and time-saving method for making the holes for transplanting seedling plants.

Glass placed over the seed box or pan, leaving a slight crack over one side to admit some air, will help to conserve the moisture, and to keep the soil moist, especially on the surface. This, however, is not nearly so essential when using peat moss as when using ordinary soil.

Give Plenty of Light. The seeds may be placed in the dark until germination takes place, but a very careful watch must be kept so that they may be removed to the light immediately upon starting through the soil. The more direct sunlight they may be given, the better. Even in partial shade, they will tend to grow up long and spindly. They should not be kept in a hot, close atmosphere, but given all the fresh air possible without bringing the temperature down below the desired point. At the same time, direct draughts of cold air should be carefully avoided.

In starting plants from seed, nothing is more important than the type of soil used. Good germination, and disease free growth thereafter, may be secured by the use of peat moss. Peat pots are ideal for plants which are to be set out later on, as there is no disturbance of the root system in the operation.

Cutting of azalea rooted in pure peat moss. Comparative growth made by coleus cutting: (left) In sand 14 days; (right) In peat moss 14 days.

Thinning Out. If the seedlings come up thickly, and there are more of them than you will want to use, *thin them out* just as soon as possible. By using tweezers, this may be done when they are still very tiny, and the remaining plants will thus have space to grow stout and stocky. Twenty five good strong plants are of more value than two hundred scrawny ones, most of which will have to be discarded at transplanting, leaving even those which are saved, of inferior quality.

The details of transplanting are described in the following chapter.

PLANTS FROM CUTTINGS

Fascinating as is the work of growing plants from seeds, there is something still more intriguing about making plants from cuttings. It gives the gardener an additional thrill to feel that his favorite geranium, or an extra dark colored or fragrant plant of heliotrope, or a petunia which among a whole batch of seedling plants, happens to be more charming than all the others, may be kept or multiplied indefinitely, by the process of taking a small part of the parent plant, and creating from it, an entirely new individual, with the exact characteristics of the old. Moreover, with peat moss as a rooting medium, many plants and shrubs which ordinarily the amateur does not attempt, may be easily and successfully propagated.

The list of plants which one may grow for himself, once the details of making and rooting cuttings have been mastered, offers indeed, a fascinating field to experiment in. Your favorite annual may be saved for another year, or new plants from them made in the autumn to be brought in the house and flowered through the winter. Your collection of house plants may be increased for your own use, or to give away to friends. From a single plant of some splendid new variety of perennial, you can have at the end of a season a dozen or more fine young specimens to replace less desirable varieties in your garden. Hedge plants, and even some of the flowering shrubs and evergreens, may be attempted as you become more expert.

How Cuttings Work. There always seems to be something more mysterious about growing plants from cuttings than about growing them from seed. That, perhaps, is one of the things which adds to the fascination of doing it. In the sense that it is not so directly in line with nature's general laws of reproduction, it *is* more mysterious.

A cutting,—or a "slip," as Grandmother used to call it—is a piece or section removed from a plant, for the purpose of obtaining a new plant of the same kind.

There are many different kinds of cuttings, but they are alike in this respect; they are all made with the idea of placing them in some sort of a medium, and under conditions, which will keep them alive until, after certain mysterious changes have taken place within the cell structure of the cutting, they will form new roots—or "strike," as it is called in technical parlance.

Just why or how this mysterious change takes place in the cell structure, enabling the plant to develop a root system at a point which normally would have remained but a piece of smooth stem, far above the ground, we do not know. But the fact remains that many plants root very readily. Recent experiments seem to indicate that there are very few which may not be so rooted, when the proper conditions to induce rooting have been discovered.

Some kinds of cuttings will start making the new root literally within a few days (see illustration of coleus cutting facing page 21.) Others require months. Preceeding the growth of the new roots, a "callus" is formed at the end of the cutting which is placed beneath the surface. The callus is a granular, scab-like formation, which is generally but not always a sign that the development of the roots will soon follow.

The conditions which are suitable to the development of root growth in the cutting are in many ways similar to those required for successful propagation from seed. The most essential factor is a sufficient and constant supply of moisture. In commercial propagation by cuttings, artificial heat is often used, but many things are grown without it. There are many plants which the amateur can successfully attempt without artificial heat. Shade, and a confined atmosphere, to maintain a moist or humid condition around the cuttings, he can supply without difficulty. This was the purpose of the glass preserve jar, inverted over slips of roses or other plants, in the old-time garden.

The factors which heretofore it has been most difficult for

the amateur worker to provide satisfactorily, have been moisture control, and a sterile medium in which to have the cuttings remain while the new roots were forming—for there are several fungus diseases which seem to be always ready to attack cuttings, especially those of soft wooded plants such as geraniums, causing decay just at the surface of the soil. I have had to throw away thousands of cuttings of geraniums and other greenhouse plants thus fatally injured even while they were forming their new root systems in the cutting bed.

This black-rot or stem-rot develops more rapidly when the surface must be watered frequently. For this reason, geraniums and other plants especially susceptible to it are often kept quite dry when being rooted in sand. This means that it takes them much longer to root. Even though so little as one fourth or one third peat moss is added to the sand, more leaves may be left upon the cuttings and rooting will take place rapidly, giving the disease less chance. Most of the ericaceous plants, such as azaleas, root best in pure peat moss. In fact, the nurseries which specialize in this class of plants, are more and more finding granulated peat moss invaluable for this purpose.

In special cases, peat moss and sand, or peat moss and soil mixtures may be used to advantage in rooting cuttings. Begonias, geraniums, and most other soft wooded plants, and viburnums and some other hard wooded plants, root more readily in peat moss and sand mixtures. Box roots rapidly in a half peat moss half soil mixture. Some azaleas, especially the Kurume types, will likewise root in this mixture. Under such conditions the cuttings can remain indefinitely in the mixture after they have rooted. The recent successes with peat moss sand and peat moss soil mixtures—in which sometimes 25% but more often 50% of peat moss is used—for certain kinds of cuttings, have resulted in their being much more extensively used.

Preparing the Rooting Medium. A flower pot, a bulb pan, an ordinary garden "flat," or a small frame, somewhat like a miniature coldframe made up on the ground, in a shaded protected location, may be used by the amateur for rooting cuttings, where only a few are to be handled at a time. The rooting medium, either pure peat moss, or peat moss mixed with soil or sand, as the case may be, should be placed to a depth of three inches or more, care being taken, of course to provide good drainage. Where a pot or a bulb pan is being used, this may be placed in a saucer, which, if kept half filled with water, will supply moisture constantly to the rooting medium in the proper amount for most cuttings. Where this is done, it will hardly ever be necessary to shade the cuttings, excepting from intense sunlight during mid-day, for the first few days.

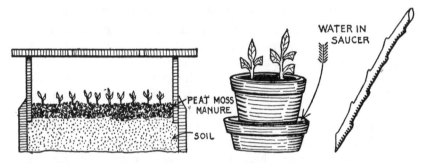

It is easy to do your own propagating with your own shrubs and plants. A small temporary frame, with a window or sash for cover, may be made out of doors; a few cuttings may be started in a pot, kept moist in a saucerful of water; or hard-wood cuttings may be made during the winter months.

Preparing the Cuttings. Cuttings of soft wooded plants, such as geraniums or begonias, are usually made two to four inches in length. Fairly firm wood, which will "snap" like a string bean when it is bent, should be selected. The leaves are removed from the lower portions, and if those remaining are large, they should be trimmed somewhat. This lessens the amount of evaporation through the leaves. The cuttings, placed close together, are inserted from a third to a half their length in the rooting medium.

Cuttings of shrubby plants, such as climbing roses and many of the flowering shrubs, may readily be rooted. The cuttings of these plants may be made either from the "green" or growing wood, in late spring or summer, or from dormant wood in fall or winter. The former are made similarly to the soft wood cuttings, and the latter are usually cut six to ten inches long, from well ripened new wood about the thickness of a lead pencil. These are tied in small bundles and placed for the winter in soil, sand, or, better still, moderately moist peat

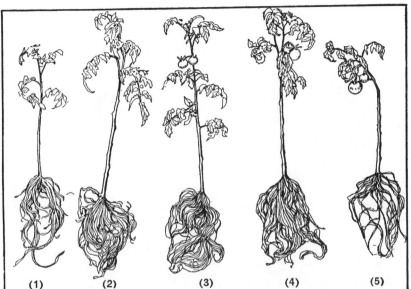

(1)   (2)   (3)   (4)   (5)

Check experiment showing how well peat moss fits into the scheme of plant nutrition. These tomatoes were grown in pots containing only: (1) acid sand; (2) building sand; (3) peat moss; (4) peat moss mixed with calcium carbonate to neutralize it; (5) garden soil. (Drawings made from photograph.)

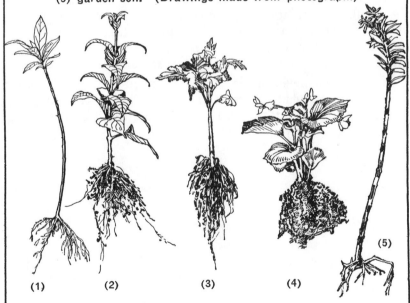

(1)   (2)   (3)   (4)   (5)

Cuttings rooted in peat moss or peat moss-sand mixtures. Note successful root development: (1) Ilex Verticillata; (2) Petunia; (3) Chrysanthemum; (4) Begonia; (5) Taxus.

Soft-wood cuttings of several varieties, showing the larger leaves trimmed back to reduce the amount of evaporation.

moss in the cellar; or in a perfectly drained location out of doors, where they may be kept until spring. By this time, they will have formed a callus, and are then placed in the rooting medium, or in some instances, with easily rooted kinds, such as California Privet, directly in the soil out of doors.

As with propagating from seed, the sterile qualities and the peculiar stimulation of root growth possessed by peat moss are of tremendous advantage in rooting cuttings. Even if you have had some success in using sand, you will find the work much easier and more certain when peat moss is employed.

If you have never made plants from cuttings, try rooting some in granulated peat moss, and see what a tremendously interesting new field of garden opportunities this interesting work opens up to you.

Tomatoes from the author's vegetable garden, within a few rods of the sea. The roots of the plant below measured over six feet across, not counting the ends that broke off in the soil. Several quarts of peat moss used in each "hill."

The author's vegetable garden referred to in the text, built upon sand without the use of top soil. Peat moss played a most important part in its success. The lower photograph was taken a few weeks after the upper one.

CHAPTER IV

PLANTING AND TRANSPLANTING

It has been estimated on reliable authority, that less than ten percent of all the trees, shrubs, and perennials which are set out by amateur gardeners in the United States, ever survive to give the satisfaction which they should to the home owners whose grounds they were designed to make more beautiful or more fruitful.

Of this astonishing percentage of failures, a very large proportion do not even get a start—never recover from the effects of poor transplanting, which is the result of carelessness or of ignorance.

In the latter case, of course, it may not really be the fault of the planter—but that does not save the tree or plant. There always will be a high percentage of loss from adverse conditions, insects, diseases, and accidents. But losses through improper methods of transplanting could be cut down to a very insignificant fraction of what they usually are. Even when plants have a strong and vigorous start, there are risks enough ahead of them. But when they are handicapped at the beginning with a poor start, barely pulling through alive, it is small wonder that they succumb to all sorts of other troubles later on.

On the other hand, if they are given a proper start, enabling them to quickly become firmly established in their new setting, and to begin vigorous growth, they are in much better shape to survive all of these other ills which plants are heir to.

The One Great Cause of Failure—Lack of Moisture

The facts and figures given in the preceeding chapters all bore witness to the fact that moisture in the soil is a most important factor in successful plant growth.

If this is true of a well established and growing plant, with roots reaching far out and far down into the soil, *then it is doubly or trebly so of the newly sprouted seedling, which must find its living within an inch or so of the surface, and of the*

27

*newly set-out plant, which has lost anywhere from 50 to 90%
of its small feeding rootlets in the process of transplanting.*

A plant, as we have seen, is a living organism. If one stops
to consider, it is easy to realize what a serious shock it must
be to the entire system of the plant to undergo a "major operation" such as transplanting, and then have to recover, not
within the protected walls of a hospital, but in the open, exposed to the elements.

Preparing the Soil to Yield a Constant Moisture Supply

It should be evident to anyone who has followed the pages
of this book thus far that anything which may be added to the
soil to increase its capacity for absorbing and holding moisture
must be of direct benefit in getting the plant established. Digging and pulverizing the soil itself, until it is fine and mellow,
will greatly increase its capacity for holding moisture. The
finer the soil particles, the greater is the exterior surface which
they present. Therefore the greater is the amount of water
held in a given quantity of soil, as the soil moisture forms
in a thin film over these surfaces. The maintainance of a
finely pulverized condition of the surface of the soil—which
is often called a "dust mulch"—will also help in conserving
the soil moisture, because it checks materially the evaporation
from the *surface* of the soil. These are facts which the reader
has probably already learned from other sources.

But even the best of garden soil, as we have already seen,
ranks very far below peat moss in its capacity for absorption
and retention of moisture. The addition of peat moss to the
soil not only improves its mechanical condition, enabling the
soil itself to retain more water, but it also *adds to the soil* a
series of tiny tanks or reservoirs, which store up water far
beyond the capacity of the best of soils to hold.

It is true that manure will help materially so far as soil
moisture is concerned. But there are many times when it is
not advisable to use manure, as for instance, in the planting of
bulbs or evergreens, and the sowing of very fine seed. Manure
is apt to bring in injurious bacteria; when exposed to the surface it is likely to dry out in hard lumps; it is not fine enough
to make an ideal bed for the smallest seed. If manure is allowed
to decay until it can be pulverized, a great deal of its fertiliz-

ing value will be lost. The nitrogen, especially, will escape in ammonia fumes and through leaching. The most effective way of using manure, incidentally, is to compost it, with a layer of peat moss below and above. Thus both the juices, containing the rich fertilizer elements, and the escaping ammonia, are saved, as peat moss has the peculiar capacity of absorbing and holding ammonia.

The addition of granulated peat moss will put the soil in an ideal condition both for planting and for transplanting. There is no danger of using too much. It cannot possibly burn or rot the roots. For soil to be used in small quantities, such as the preparation of a coldframe or a hotbed, or a made-up bed for sowing fine seeds in the open, 25 to 50% in bulk of peat moss may well be added to the upper three or four inches of soil. For larger areas, it may be spread on evenly in layer from one to four inches deep, and dug in. On light sandy soil, it is well to dig the peat well *beneath* the surface. On such soils, extremely quick drainage tends to carry off and waste the fertilizing elements. The peat moss acts as a trap to catch and hold these escaping plant foods, and to save them for the roots which will find them later. On heavy or clay soils, on the contary, it is best to keep the peat moss fairly *near the surface,* where it can absorb and hold the moisture before it runs off, and also to keep the surface soil from caking or crusting.

Planting

The general preparation of the soil, combined with the information contained in the previous chapter on propagating plants from seed, indicates the method of soil preparation for the planting of seed.

For sowing seeds in very light sandy soil, almost pure sand, I have found it very helpful to open up a furrow and distribute two or three inches of granulated peat moss along the row, covering this lightly with soil and sowing the seeds directly on top. This has served to give the plants a strong start under extremely adverse conditions. My vegetable garden for the last two years, has been made on soil which is so near pure sand that I would not have attempted to handle it without the use of peat moss.

For transplanting, the peat moss may be mixed with the soil in the hole where the plant is to be set, or a mixture of half soil and half peat moss made for filling in around the roots of the plant. I employed both of these methods this past spring in planting a garden which had to be established on ground that had been filled in with beach-sand, and which, although a considerable amount of top-soil was added, I would have considered "impossible" if it had not been for my previous experience with peat moss under just such adverse conditions. The photograph facing page 27 is a view of this garden, taken about ten weeks after it had been planted.

In the transplanting of evergreens, particularly, the generous use of peat moss in the holes has given results astonishing even to the most experienced planters. This is touched upon further in chapter VII.

A method sometimes successfully used in setting out very small plants with bare roots, is to hold a layer of moist peat moss in one hand, place the plant roots upon it, add more peat moss, and squeeze the whole into a cone-shaped ball which then may readily be planted. This is especially to be recommended in setting out plants in very dry soil under adverse conditions. Roots are quickly formed in the ball of moist peat moss which keeps the plant "fresh" until the roots re-establish themselves.

The use of peat moss should not make one less careful about following out good planting practices, such as thoroughly firming the surface on top of seeds planted in dry soil; and packing the earth carefully and very tightly about the roots of plants, trees, or shrubs, when they are set out.

So far as the employment of water is concerned, either for moistening the soil in transplanting or for irrigating, the use of peat moss merely means that *more* water, rather than less, may be applied, because the saturation point will not be reached nearly so quickly as with soil which does not contain any peat moss. A muddy condition, resulting possibly in a dry, hard cake later on, will be avoided. The length of the intervals between waterings may be doubled, and often trebled. In other words, plants set out in soil containing a generous proportion of peat moss merely means that *more* water, rather than less, than would otherwise be the case.

Transplanting

The general principles which apply to transplanting are naturally much the same as those associated with planting. The chief difference is that in transplanting, we are working with living plants in a state of active growth, and that therefore the roots should be protected at all times from drying out.

Transplanting Seedlings. To go back to the little seedling plants which we left safely started in the preceeding chapter, the first question is to decide when they should be moved, or transplanted, from the seedbed to new quarters.

As a fairly general rule, we may say "the earlier the better." The smaller the plants, the bigger the proportion of the root system which can be taken up and saved with the plant in transplanting. In any transplanting, not matter how carefully it may be done, a large percentage of the root system must be lost. This destroys the balance, or equilibrium, between the top and the root-system of the plant, which has been established in its development. The top, therefore, does not receive from the roots the full supply of water which it has been getting. The plant cells, being but partially filled with water, begin to collapse. This is what causes "wilting." If conditions are favorable, a new root-system is quickly developed, the tops revive, and the plant goes on growing as though nothing had happened. It is evident, therefore, that the two objects to be aimed at in transplanting are, first, to maintain as nearly as possible the water supply from the roots to the top; and secondly, to decrease the amount of moisture which the tops will require. The latter purpose is accomplished sometimes by reducing the top of the plant, (trimming back large leaves, or, in the case of larger plants, pruning back the plant) ; and also by maintaining a humid atmosphere around the transplanted plant.

With small seedling plants, reducing the top of the plant will not be necessary. It does help, however, to keep seedling plants shaded from bright sunshine, and to give them an occasional light syringing, for a few days after transplanting.

Soil for Transplanting. Most soil for seedlings or small plants may be made by mixing up good garden loam and granulated peat moss, half and half. If some old, thoroughly decomposed manure is available, it will be an excellent material to add to this mixture. I use also a small amount of fine bone flour and tankage, mixed half and half. A four or five inch pot full of the fertilizer to a bushel of soil mixture is sufficient.

The little seedlings may be given a "first shift" either to flats, about 3″ deep, or to small pots. Remove them from the seed bed gently, to damage the roots as little as possible, and plant them somewhat deeper than they originally grew, so that the stems will be well supported. Be sure to make a hole— with the forefinger or with a small stick—sufficiently large to take the roots in a natural position, without crowding. With the tips of the thumbs and forefingers, press the soil very firmly about the roots—not merely against the stems on the surface.

Transplanting Larger Plants. As the little plants grow they may need to be shifted to larger pots. This should be done when the roots have formed a mat around the inside of the pot, as indicated in one of the accompanying cuts. Usually it is best to change to a pot only one or two sizes larger

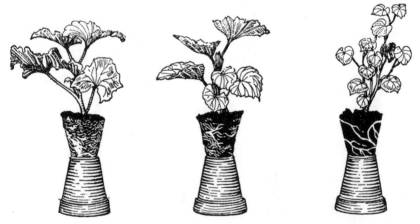

Repotting plants growing in pots. In drawing at right, the roots have not yet developed sufficiently. In center, they are ready for repotting; at left, they have been allowed to remain too long, resulting in the plant becoming "potbound."

than that in which the plant has been growing. A little larger proportion of soil may be added to the potting mixture to give it more body. As before, the plant should be kept from wilting as much as possible for the first few days after being potted. With the new peat-pots, made from compressed peat moss, which are now available, transplanting is much simplified, as the plant is allowed to remain in the pot, *pot and all being planted*. Thus there is no disturbance whatsoever of the root system. The peat-pot gradually decomposes in the soil, providing additional plant food and humus.

Transplanting In The Open. There is very little difficulty in transplanting to the open ground plants which have been grown in pots, as the ball of roots remains more or less intact. If the peat-pots described above are used, even those things which are most difficult to transplant, as for instance cucumbers and melons or phlox and delphinums may be set out without the slightest danger of loss.

Seedling plants, which have been growing in a frame or in a seed-bed, and are to be transplanted to their permanent position, without having been previously transplanted, are more difficult. Each time a plant is transplanted, a dense mass of fiberous roots is formed, thus making each suceeding transplanting safer. Seedling plants, therefore, should be shifted to their permanent position as soon as practicable. If they are large and soft, and likely to wilt badly, it is much better to cut the plants back a third to a half. With many annuals and perennials, particularly those which are inclined to make a single main stem,—such as snapdragons or hardy carnations—this will be an advantage in any event, as it induces a stocky, bushy growth, as well as preventing wilting at the time of transplanting. If the weather is hot and bright, a few sheets of newspaper placed over the newly transplanted plants, and held in position by small stones or a few handfuls of earth, will help to maintain a more humid atmosphere around the plant.

After Care. After the plants are set out, everything possible should be done to maintain the soil moisture. The incorporation of plenty of peat moss, when transplanting, will of course help to do this, as already explained.

The surface of the soil should never be allowed to get hard. Cultivate or hoe frequently around the newly set out plants to maintain a surface soil mulch. Where the plants are set out in rows in the garden, this may be done very quickly and efficiently with the garden rake.

In the flower borders, or around individual shrubs, plants, or trees, a mulch of peat moss, two to three inches thick, will go far toward assuring a satisfactory growth through periods of dry weather. Such a mulch may well be applied as a general practice, when hot weather comes in June. It helps to keep down weed growth, gives the beds a most attractive dressy appearance, and if watering is necessary, the mulch will make every gallon applied accomplish as much as would two or three gallons without the mulch.

Oh happy garden, in May air
With lawns and wilding arbours fair,
And paths of springing green
Save of nesting birds unseen.
Listen, and tell of love as they
When youth is youth and May is May.

The lawn makes or mars the beauty of the landscape; and the character of the soil makes or mars the beauty of the lawn.

CHAPTER V

LAWNS

As a suitable setting magnifies the beauty of a fine gem, so a good lawn increases the attractiveness of a fine residence. And so far as the landscape planting is concerned, it has been stated with a good deal of truth, that "the lawn makes it or mars it."

The essentials of a good lawn are three: it should be correctly graded; it should possess a smooth and uniform surface; and it should remain permanently green.

Even an amateur knows what he wants to get in a lawn. But nine out of ten beginners make the great mistake of assuming that the success of the lawn depends almost entirely upon the kind of seed they use. If the results of a first attempt are not successful, then the remedy employed is to try a different seedsman, whose lawn-grass mixture bears a different name or brand. A good lawn-grass mixture may be bought from any reliable seedsman. The weight of the mixture is sometimes an idication of the quality of the seed; but this, of course, does not hold if the weight is obtained by using a surplus of clover, which is much heavier for its bulk than grass seed. A good general purpose lawn grass seed should weigh not less than 20 pounds per bushel, without a high percentage of clover. In lawn making, it is now the practice to use less clover then formerly, and a more acid reacting soil, which is unfavorable to many of the weeds developing in a "sweet" soil, such as clover likes best. Much of the liming of lawns that is done, is not only unnecessary but may be a disadvantage rather than an advantage. Liming should be resorted to only when the soil is truly sour, as indicated by the development of green moss, and the presence of an abnormal number of earth worms, and even then, not oftener than once in three years.

Creeping bent and fescue grasses are being used more and more in lawn making, and for turf which has to stand an unusual amount of wear, such as putting greens and tennis courts. These grasses thrive best in a slightly acid reacting soil. Also, lawns and pleasure turfs of creeping bent are now often made by planting the "stolons" or pieces of the creeping roots. In either instance peat moss is particularly valuable in making a lawn where these grasses are to be used. Peat moss supplies the necessary acid condition, and keeps the surface of the soil moist, enabling the stolons to re-root quickly, and making it possible to secure a dense, smooth, tough turf in a shorter time than by any other known method.

The fact of the matter is that nine-tenths of the success of the lawn depends upon what is done *before* a single seed is sown. Remember that you are asking of the plants which will make up your lawn that they shall grow under conditions which most plants would not survive. Practically no cultivation is possible; and yet a mulch, which is often used to take the place of cultivation, cannot be employed. Watering can be done, of course, but only under unfavorable conditions. Without either cultivation or a mulch, the water is rapidly wasted again by drainage and by excessive surface evaporation.

Under these circumstances, it is small wonder that the beginner frequently has more trouble with his lawn than with any feature of his home ground planting. What, then, is the answer?

Building For a Permanent Lawn

The first step towards establishing a satisfactory lawn is to secure the correct grading. This item is foreign to our present discussion, excepting to point out that the owner should watch carefully to see that the "rough grading," which is often done with very poor, gravelly soil, should not be brought at any point too near what will be the surface of the finish grade. Personally, I would much rather have the rough grading done with ashes or with soft cinders (not hard cinders or clinkers) than with poor soil. The ashes themselves make a good moisture holder and contain some plant food, especially potash. Many grasses make a particularly vigorous root growth when they can get hold of ashes in the soil.

The fertilizers used in starting a lawn should be generous in quantity, and of a character which will supply both the immediate needs of the young plants, and the hungry roots later in the season, and even the following year. Fine bone meal, and very coarse bone meal, mixed, will yield a long and continuous supply of prosphoric acid. Nitrate of soda, tankage, and cotton-seed meal, in equal parts, will provide available nitrogen throughout the entire season. Synthetic nitrogen (Urea) mixed with peat moss as a carrier, in the proportions of one to twelve by weight, is equally desirable.

Humus In The Soil. The most generous supply of plant food in the soil being prepared for seeding a lawn, however, will avail nothing beyond temporary immediate results, unless the soil is also well supplied with humus to maintain a constant moisture supply. It is a poor policy to depend upon daily sprinklings. Aside from the cost and the inconvenience, this produces the growth of the roots at the very surface of the soil. For a strong, tough, and permanent lawn, the roots should be induced to go as deep as possible. If a generous supply of peat moss is used, and this, together with the fertilizer, is mixed well through the soil to a depth of three or four inches, the foundation for a strong, permanent lawn will have been laid, and a minimum of watering will be required to keep it in good thriving condition.

Sowing. If after this preliminary preparation, the surface is raked fine and smooth like a table top, a generous amount of good seed used, the surface thoroughly rolled, and then carefully watered with a very fine spray, so as not to wash any of the seed, a good lawn, which will begin to show fairly green within four or five weeks, should result. A temporary wire fence can be used to protect the surface wherever there is any danger of its being stepped on before the turf has formed.

Repairing and Renovating the Lawn. Aside from accident, and actual abuse, the biggest cause of a lawn's becoming spotty and moth eaten in appearance, is the uneven nourishment of the plants of which it is composed. It may, for instance, usually be noticed early in the life of a lawn that some spots will "dry out" much quicker than others. Lacking moisture in the soil, even if the fertilizers have been evenly distributed, the plants at these places do not keep up with the average. This is much less likely to happen in a lawn prepared as suggested above, because the peat moss in the soil holds the rain or the irrigation *where it falls,* and thus maintains a uniform growth over the entire surface.

Much can be done to correct the uneven or spotty condition of a lawn, especially if it is taken in time, by applying a top dressing, which should be lightly raked and then thoroughly watered into the surface. The top dressing may be made of two-thirds peat moss and one-third garden loam, adding a couple of pounds of tankage, or two or three times that amount of dried sheep manure, to each bushel of the compost. The mixture should be run through a screen to get it thoroughly fine, so that when spread on, it will readily work down between the blades of grass to the roots; or here again, synthetic nitrogen (Urea) will be admirably adaptable as a stimulating fertilizer, best applied in liquid form, 1 pound to 100 gallons of water.

Bare Spots in the soil are best remedied by digging out the old sod in a square or a circle, back to an even edge of good turf. If there seems to be something wrong with the soil, remove it to a depth of four inches, and replace it with soil prepared as suggested above, under making a new lawn. If the damage is the result of some accident, this will not be necessary. Merely fill in level, with the top dressing mixture described above, and resow.

Low Spots in the lawn, or ruts, such as are made when the driver of the coal truck tries to see in how many places he can run over it before you begin shooting at him, may be remedied by gradually filling them up with the top dressing mixture, adding a little at a time, as the new growth comes up through.

Renovating a Worn-out Lawn

When·the entire lawn begins to get run down and shabby looking, it is quite a problem whether to attempt to doctor it back into shape, or to rip it up entirely and remake it. The latter course is the most drastic, but usually the most satisfactory in the end. There are, however, often many reasons for not doing this, aside from the expense involved.

The best way to bring an old lawn back without entirely remaking it, is as follows: Rake it vigorously, to remove all old, loose grass. Then go over it with an edger and a spade, cutting out clean the worst parts, as suggested above for patching. If a spiked lawn roller, which is made for this purpose, is not available, the surface may be loosened up by going over it with a tined fork, or with an extra heavy, long-toothed iron rake, such as is used for mixing concrete. Much of the old sod may be torn out, but that cannot be helped. The essential thing is to *break up the old, hard surface crust,* and to fill it full of holes. Then give it a good top dressing with bone meal, 5 to 7 pounds to each 100 square feet. If the soil is sour, apply about twice or three times this quantity of agricultural lime. Follow this up by going over the surface with the top dressing compost described above, getting it down into the holes and cracks into the soil as much as possible.

Then rake the entire surface as smooth as it can be made, and resow, using nearly as much seed as you would to make a new lawn. This treatment, of course, will involve considerable work, but is not any where near so expensive as entirely remaking the lawn, and often will produce very satisfactory results.

Keeping a Good Lawn Good. Constant watering alone is not sufficient to maintain a good lawn, as many amateurs seem to think. The plant food in the soil, no matter how much was originally put in, gradually becomes exhausted, and should be occasionally replaced by a good top dressing of bone meal, or some other suitable fertilizer. Top dressing should never be applied to a dry lawn. Put it on just after rain, or after a thorough irrigating. A slight additional sprinkling will wash it from the leaves and down into the soil.

Rolling is of benefit to most lawns, particularly early in the spring, or during periods of wet weather. Where a roller is not available, the back of the spade may often be used for firming and evening up the surface where moles have run, or where it may be necessary for other reasons, such as walking on soft, wet sod, which should never be done.

It is a mistake to keep a lawn cut too close, particularly during dry weather. The sunbaking of the surface soil between the roots is injurious. Where the turf is not so thick as it might be, and bare soil shows between the plants, sifted peat moss can be sprinkled over the surface, forming a sort of miniature mulch. While not deep, this is of decided value in checking evaporation, and keeping the roots cool.

Do not, from force of tradition, go through the disagreeable performance of covering your lawn with stable manure for the winter or spring. Unless it is very finely pulverized, the grass is almost sure to be smothered out in spots: and the plant food from the manure will be distributed very unevenly. The manure top-dressing is of some benefit to the lawn, of course, but no more than is derived as well, or better, with much greater convenience, from the use of peat moss, bone meal, and any organic fertilizer high in nitrogen, such as Urea, tankage, dried blood, or sheep manure. If you are so fortunate as to be able to obtain barnyard manure, do not place it on the front lawn; save it for the compost heap (see page 29) for the choicest flowers and vegetables.

Who loves not roses, knows not Beauty's smile;
Romance hath spurned him,—Poetry passed him by
On silver sandals in the purple night.
He stands aloof, alone, sightless and deaf, the while
Roses, red roses, voice the fond lover's cry,
Roses, white roses, from white breasts answering sigh,
Roses, all roses, bloom for the soul's delight.

—ROCKWELL

Who has not dreamed of having roses like these? There is nothing like a blanket of peat moss, summer and winter, for making dream roses materialize into real roses!

CHAPTER VI

SUCCESS WITH ROSES

The rose is unquestionably still the Queen of Flowers, although it may be doubted if her leadership in general popularity is so far above all challenge as in the past. Such flowers as the dahlia and the gladiolus now command substantial and enthusiastic followings. The shadow of rivalry, however, has not been a bad thing for the rose. It is partly as a result of this that we are now getting better roses, hardier roses, and roses which may be more easily grown than ever before.

Nevertheless, when it comes to the garden or bush roses, and especially to the hybrid-teas, which now constitute by far the most important class, it is no sinecure to grow them with complete success. There are few flowers which the amateur is more proud to bring to perfection—and none which serve as a greater reward for any pains which may be taken with them.

It is estimated by one of the country's leading rose authorities that fifteen to twenty million rose plants are sold each year. Everyone who has anything to do with this business knows what a tremendously high percentage of mortality occurs in the rose garden of the amateur. There is probably no other flower which is more anxious to keep and to succeed with, and few others which he so frequently loses.

The Three Special Uses of Peat Moss in Rose Growing

What seems to be the difficulty?

In the first place, the types of roses we want in our garden are not the ones which grow naturally under the conditions we have to offer them. Then, too, they are highly bred—like Jersey or Guernsey cattle; they are the most desirable of all, but they are not so capable of standing exposure and shifting for themselves as something more native to the conditions which are to be met. And then there is the fact that bush roses do not make a wide spreading, tenaceous and fibrous root-system such as would fit them to go foraging for themselves and to withstand drought and other adverse conditions.

41

To the grower of roses, peat moss is a boon in three distinct ways. It is invaluable for use in the preparation of the soil for the planting; it makes an ideal winter mulch for the soil surface and the protection of the rose plants themselves; and it is unequalled for summer mulching, which plays a far more important part in the successful culture of roses than of almost any other ordinary garden plant, with the possible exception of hardy lilies and some of the broad leaved evergreens. Just how well peat moss is adapted to each of these several purpose, we will endeavor to make plain.

Building a Rose Garden for Permanent Results

There is probably no popular flower concerning which so much has been written in the way of cultural directions—and none with which such directions are more generally ignored on the part of the planter. Not because he is unwilling to take pains, but because the directions given are so frequently impractical, if not wholly impossible, for the amateur gardener who is doing his own work and has a limited bank account. We are still frequently told, for instance, that the bed where roses are to be planted, should be excavated to a depth of two feet, be filled in with 6 inches of crushed stone or some similar good drainage material; have a layer of inverted sod put over this, to keep the soil from washing down through; receive next a layer 12 inches or so in depth, of a compost of heavy (preferably clay) soil, and cow manure, which has been packed in layers and allowed to remain "for a few months or a year"; and finished off with a surface soil of good clay loam. Such a bed, after it has been allowed to settle for a "few months," will be ready to receive your rose plants!

Now, there is no doubt at all that this is an excellent way to make a rose garden; or that a garden so made, other conditions being favorable, will produce splendid roses. But for how many amateur gardeners of your acquaintance is this a practical, workable prescription?

The question is whether or not there is some other method of preparing the rose garden which will give satisfactory results, but which will be easier, quicker and less expensive. I maintain that there is.

First of all, as to the matter of clay soil. This is an old tradition in rose growing. If one had to use the soil in which roses are to be planted *in its natural state,* undoubtedly a fairly heavy soil would be preferable to lighter ones. This, however, is not the case. The point I wish to make is that perfectly good roses may be grown in light soils if they are properly treated. Some of the finest garden roses I have ever seen, were growing in a light, sandy soil. One of the most beautiful rose gardens in England is on soil so sandy that it would, ordinarily, be considered entirely unsuitable for rose growing—although it is from the English gardeners that most of our rose lore, impractical for our American conditions but still passed on, has been handed down. Do not feel that you cannot grow good garden roses, even though your soil happens to be light, or even sandy.

Let us analyse, for a moment, the actual conditions produced by the elaborate preparations outlined above.

Good Drainage. First of all is *drainage.* That is essential; roses will not grow with wet feet. But in most gardens, the drainage is sufficiently good without any excavating and filling in. If the soil *is* poorly drained—so that the water remains at or near the surface after a rain—this must be remedied before you can expect to grow good roses. Digging out the soil to a depth of 10 to 12 inches, thoroughly loosening the subsoil with a pickaxe, and filling in with several inches of coal ashes, will usually remedy this condition. I have found coal ashes preferable to broken stone or similar material because, while allowing the surplus water to drain through quite as readily, they also retain and hold for future use a large amount of moisture. They are, of course, easier to obtain; you can usually procure them from your own cellar. But ordinarily, in a soil adapted to most perennials, roses may be grown without any excavating.

Long Lasting Food Supplies. Undoubtedly, there is no better plant food for roses than well rotted cow manure: it contains nitrogen, and the other elements needed, and unlike horse manure, it lasts a long time, the plant food becoming "available" (see page 10) evenly, over a long period. Also it is a great moisture holder; and roses, to a greater extent than most perennials or shrubs, are in a constant state of growth, from early April to October or November, and so are in a particular need of a constant supply of soil moisture.

Moisture in the Soil. It is chiefly for the purpose of maintaining the constant supply of soil moisture that the decayed sod, so universally recommended for rose garden making is used; the rotted turf supplies excellent humus, in which the rose roots revel.

Making a Rose Garden With Peat Moss. Cow manure and heavy loam turf, however, while they were plentiful on the old English estates whose private gardeners gave us our first directions for rose-bed making, are not so easily available to the average suburban garden owner. Fortunately, in granulated peat moss, he has an inexpensive and immediately ready-to-use form of humus which is capable of absorbing much more moisture than the best of decayed turf sod. Dried, prepared shredded cow manure may be obtained for mixing with this, if one feels that cow manure is essential; personally, I do not feel that it is, for I have seen excellent roses grown without it, and have myself obtained satisfactory results with a mixture of tankage, cotton seed meal, fine bone and very coarse bone, or horn shavings, in equal parts. This gives supplies of nitrogen and phosphoric acid which will gradually become available over a long period. As a source of potash for roses, I prefer tobacco fertilizer to anything else I have ever used. The mixture of fertilizers described above may be applied at the rate of 4 to 6 pounds for each 100 square feet, and the tobacco fertilizer at the same rate, in addition. This is a heavier application than that which would be used for most garden purposes, but roses are hungry feeders and this supply of food is designed to last over into the second season.

Preparing The Bed For Planting. A good rose garden may be made by spading up the bed, broadcasting the fertilizer, applying a 3 or 4 inch layer of peat moss, and forking this into the soil as thoroughly as possible. It is better, however, to entirely remove 5 or 6 inches of soil, fork in the fertilizer and peat moss, in the layer *beneath* this, and then to fill in the top with sifted soil, to which about 25% in bulk of peat moss has been added. This is but little more work than the other method and is well worth the additional trouble because the moisture and plant food will be well below the surface, in-

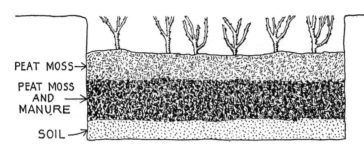

PEAT MOSS→

PEAT MOSS
AND →
MANURE

SOIL→

An easy and effective way of preparing the rose bed for planting which assures getting the plant food well below the surface, thus inducing deep rooting; for details, see text.

ducing the roses to root deeply. The fine soil at the surface makes easy planting, and furnishes a soil mulch: such a bed will absorb and hold an extraordinary amount of water, yet the soil will not puddle on the surface after heavy rains, and will not become packed. If the soil is prepared as recommended above, it will not be necessary to keep the bed so narrow that one can tend to and cut the roses "without stepping into the bed,"—another of the old, handed down, rose garden traditions.

The method of making a rose garden suggested above, may be carried out without undue expense or labor; the beds will be ready for planting just as soon as finished; and roses set out in them will make a strong, vigorous start, and continue in good growth for a long time.

Care of the Rose Garden

No matter how carefully any rose garden is made however, it will not continue to produce good roses unless the plants receive adequate care. They will require more attention than most perennials, bulbs or shrubs.

Cultivation. Immediately after the rose garden is planted, which will have resulted in more or less trampling upon and consequently packing down of the soil, the surface should be lightly loosened up with a pronged hoe, which will go to a depth of 3 or 4 inches, and *then* raked over on the surface to establish the "soil mulch."

The soil between rose bushes should never be allowed to become packed hard, or to form a crust; hoe, cultivate and

45

rake as frequently as may be necessary to keep the soil mellow for three inches or so in depth, and finely pulverized on the surface; that is the first step towards success.

Pruning. Garden roses require more careful attention in the way of pruning than any other class of plants in the home garden. They should be cut back quite severely when planted. This is for the double purpose of reducing evaporation, and of stimulating growth of *new* wood, upon which the flowers will be produced.

Another light pruning or trimming back may be given after the June flowering period; this should not be a severe pruning. If the roses have been cut heavily, it may not be necessary at all; otherwise, the most vigorous of the new branches or canes may be cut back a quarter to a third; as this will have a tendency to increase the amount of the fall bloom. Again, late in the fall—just before freezing weather—exceptionally vigorous canes, which would be likely to whip about in the wind, may be cut back a half or more. The most important pruning, however, is done in the spring. All dead and very weak wood should be removed entirely, and the remaining canes cut back to from three or four, to twice that number, of buds. The more severe the pruning, the better will be the individual blooms, but there will not be so many of them.

Top-dressing. Early in the spring of the second season, and each succeeding spring, the roses should be supplied with additional plant food in the form of a well balanced fertilizer. Personally, I like the mixture suggested above for planting time as well as any I have ever used for this annual top dressing. Another desirable mixture is bone meal and sheep manure. These are all animal fertilizers, and there is no danger of burning the roots with them. They should be worked into the soil as deeply as possible without injuring the roots. Watch growth of your roses carefully at all times and whenever they do not seem to be growing as vigorously as they should, give a light application of nitrate of soda, dried blood, or Urea, or bone flour. Liquid cow manure is excellent, but not always procurable. Nitrogenous fertilizer should *not* be applied late in the autumn, as this stimulates a soft growth which does not have a chance to mature before freezing weather and is subject to injury.

46

Summer Mulching. Where the summers are hot, during long dry spell, roses are likely to be checked, no matter how frequently or carefully the soil may be cultivated. A summer mulch of peat moss applied just before the roses come into bloom, will hold the moisture in the soil and take the shock of the hot sun from the roots and lessen troublesome weeding, and prevent the surface from baking or crusting.

Dr. J. Horace MacFarland, editor of the American Rose Annual, and one of the country's leading rose authorities, has this to say concerning mulching with peat moss:

"My continued use of Granulated Peat Moss under the rose plantings at Breeze Hill confirms my earlier feeling as to its real value, and I have no hesitancy in commending its use.

The mulch seems to check the growth of weeds, surely reducing the necessity for cultivation, keeps the surface of the ground under it moist and open, and adds a really attractive appearance to the rose-beds. As I stir it in each spring in the rough shale with which I have to deal, the texture of the ground is improved."

Captain Thomas, another nationally known rose authority, says:

"Mulches are a form of protection which is most valuable in the retention of moisture and which also cuts down the labor of cultivation and weeding. Peat moss, spread to a depth of 2 inches, after being finely ground, is the best mulch."

Winter Mulching. The unusual efficiency of peat moss for winter mulching has already been explained (see page 4). The purpose of most winter mulching is not to keep the soil from freezing, but to maintain it in a frozen condition. In the winter mulching of roses, however, we have a further objective. In the northern states, many of the garden roses, particularly the hybrid teas and teas, are likely to be killed back almost to the ground if they do not receive some protection. If the soil is mounded up well about the stems, in much the same way that one hills corn, just before the ground freezes, and a three inch mulch of peat moss is added *after* the soil freezes,

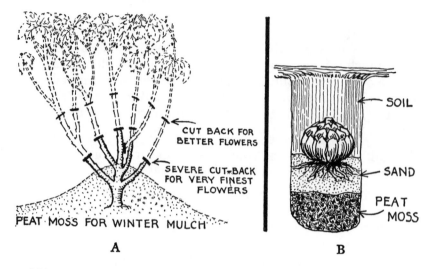

CUT BACK FOR
BETTER FLOWERS

SEVERE CUT-BACK
FOR VERY FINEST
FLOWERS

PEAT MOSS FOR WINTER MULCH

A

SOIL

SAND

PEAT
MOSS

B

(A) Two of the most important points in rose garden culture are winter mulching and spring pruning; for details and further information, see text.

(B) Method of planting hardy lilies; sand immediately around and below the bulb keeps the scales dry and free from decay; peat moss below the sand supplies the moisture and humus in which the new roots revel.

adequate protection will be given; the peat moss serves not only to protect the base of the stems, but keeps the soil frozen until late in spring and guards against the possibility of premature growth. The peat moss mulching may then be worked into the soil during the early spring cultivating.

If you are a lover of garden roses, you will find as I have found, that granulated peat moss is one of the greatest helps in their culture.

48

The garden trees are busy with the shower
That fell ere sunset; now methinks they talk,
Lowly and sweetly, as befits the hour
One to another down the grassy walk . . . . .
That with May dawn their leaves may be o'erflowed,
And dews about their feet may never fail.

—HALLAM

Helpful to most plants, peat moss is almost indispensable for the broad-leaved evergreens, such as rhododendrons (see inset), laurel, azaleas, and other ericaceous sorts; and it accomplishes wonders in the transplanting of coniferous evergreens.

CHAPTER VII

EVERGREENS AND EVERGREEN SHRUBS

Undoubtedly the one big reason why we all love evergreens, is to be found in the word itself. There is something akin to inspiration as well as good cheer in these stalwart knights of the plant world who, with lances lifted to the sky, continue successfully to defy the crushing hand of winter, that has long since stripped all other things of their greenery, and left even the noblest oak or the widest spreading elm but a tangle of twigs,

"Upon those boughs which shake against the cold,
Bare ruined choirs, where late the sweet birds sang."

From my window, as I write, I can see a little group of small redcedars. They were inconspicuous enough when I first set them out last autumn; but now they dominate not only the corner of the garden which they occupy, but all of the open space within sight. Not another green thing is visible except the few leaves which still cling in the thicket of honeysuckle back of them—and a bit farther north, even those would be missing. I know, of course, that the trees back of them, and the bulbs planted at their feet, will come to life again with returning spring; but nevertheless, it is very comforting to be able to look out and see them still green and happy on the bleakest winter morning; and if the night has brought a fall of snow, it merely serves to make them more beautiful than ever.

No garden is complete without some evergreens. Even if one does not possess a garden at all, in the fuller sense of the word, evergreens in the foundation planting around the house will serve to maintain an atmosphere of cheerfulneess and comfort which nothing else in the way of plants can possibly yield.

The "Secrets" of Success with Evergreens

All evergreens, while they submit to the captivity of our gardens, are and remain more or less things of the wild. Many

49

of our garden favorites, such as the dahlia, gladiolus, and the rose, bear slight resemblance to their original form. But the evergreens, for the most part, have been merely captured, never domesticated. Even the numerous varieties are, almost without exception, merely variations of the natural types which have been perpetuated by vegetative propagation (Pages 21 to 26)

If, then, we are to succeed with evergreens, it is logical that we should attempt to give them so far as possible conditions similar to those under which they naturally grow.

Some spruces, such as the white spruce, will stand a dry and windy climate better than others, though all of them do best where there is a fair degree of moisture in the atmosphere. We will not select a hemlock to plant in a dry situation exposed to the full sun; nor a mugho pine for a moist shady spot.

But aside from these general considerations, what can we do? If we take the trouble to investigate the conditions under which evergreens naturally grow, we find them *not* so particular as to soil, thriving over areas including many widely divergent types: but there is always excellent drainage—they are hillside growers. And even where they go down to rivers or lakes, there is never water standing about the roots; the exceptions, such as the white or swamp-cedar, may be counted on the fingers of one hand. And all of the evergreens, as they grow naturally, are almost always heavily *mulched* with a layer of their own needlees, the accumulation of year after year, in various stages of decomposition. Dig down into the humus-mat with your fingers, even on a hot day, and you will find it cool and moist above the network of spreading roots.

Coming to the evergreen shrubs—the broadleaved evergreens—such as laurels, rhododendrons, azaleas, inkberry, and even the little ground plants, like partridge berries, and arbutus, we find them quite uniform in their preferences, which include shady or at least sheltered locations, and a peaty, acid reacting soil. If we expect these to do well in our gardens, we must cater to their tastes.

Planting and Care of Coniferous Evergreens

There are two reasons why evergreens are particularly difficult to transplant successfully. The first is that there is no period of the year when they are not evaporating or trans-piring a great amount of moisture. Unlike the deciduous trees and shrubs, they do not obligingly shed all their leaves for us, automatically curtailing the demand for moisture which the tops make upon the roots, and giving us an excellent opportunity to transplant them. (See page 53). One cannot well cut or prune them back in order to keep the tops in proportion to the roots without injuring or at least disfiguring them. Fortunately, as far as the home gardener is concerned, this difficulty has brought about its own remedy: for evergreens are so hard to transplant, that they are now almost universally shipped "B & B."—that is with a ball of earth and roots held firmly in a burlap wrapping.

Even with this precaution, however, transplanting is not always successful, though they may survive for six months or a year after they are put in the ground. Once ever-greens are well established, their roots will run great distances to find and utilize sources of moisture. But for the first few years, they must be dependent wholly upon that which is available in the immediate vicinity of the tree. The benefits of the generous use of peat moss in planting, or in transplanting evergreens, is perhaps more striking than with any other group of plants. I have planted them on the lightest of soils, and under the most adverse conditions, and obtained splendid results. In transplanting collected native sorts from the woods peat moss has given, in several instances of which I know, an almost incredible percentage of success. Commercial evergreen grow-ers are using it more and more extensively and enthusiastically. The critical point in evergreen transplanting is to get the *new* root growth started. Peat moss seems to accomplish this in a wonderful way, in addition to its merit as a moisture holder. Last autumn I had occasion to move an old moss cypress which, through neglect and from growing almost under an arborvitae, seemed next to worthless—so poor that if it had not been for my wife's protest, it would have been committed to the dump without more ado. I looked at most to see it pull through the winter alive, and possibly make an effort to start in the spring. To my great surprise, within three months it had made new growth, and was so greatly improved as to be hardly recog-nizable as the same plant. I feel certain that without the peat moss that was used, it would have been fortunate to have survived at all. The following quotation from a letter from a prominent commercial grower voices the experience which many others have had.

"My method of planting rhododendrons is with peat moss used liberally, mixed with about an equal amount of soil, and then the hose turned on at time of planting, washing the material into close contact with the roots. The results have been remarkable. With the use of peat moss we think nothing of receiving a carload of rhododendrons, healing them in roughly in peat moss and allowing them to stand without further attention other than the original watering for six or eight weeks. In fact our healing in ground is composed almost entirely of peat moss, and in this ground we heal in cedars, laurels, azaleas, etc., without fear of loss."

Mulching. Until an evergreen is several years old and has had a chance to accumulate its own needle mulch, a peat moss mulch will be found of the greatest benefit. If planting has been done in the fall, this should be applied when the ground freezes, taking care to soak the ground thoroughly *before* freezing, if there has not been plenty of rain. This winter mulch for the first two seasons may well be worked into the soil in the spring, so as to keep the ground mellow and to destroy any weeds which may start. At the advent of hot weather, a *summer* mulch applied in the same way, will be equally beneficial, and will help in conserving such water as it may be necessary to apply, if the season is a dry one.

Staking. One of the greatest causes of loss of newly planted evergreens, is the swaying of the trees by the wind, which moves the roots just enough to interfere greatly with their getting etsablished in their new quarters. All evergreens of good size should be firmly supported by being tied to stakes in two, and better three, directions. It is a little more trouble to do this, but may save many expensive specimens and all the trouble in the time and disappointment in replanting.

Planting and Care of Broadleaved Evergreens

The same difficulties in planting which attend the coniferous evergreens are involved in the handling of the broadleaved sorts, and they may be overcome in the same way.

52

Location and Soil. For the broadleaved evergreens, as may be supposed from the remarks concerning their natural conditions of growth, a somewhat sheltered location should be selected. They are often planted at the edge of woods; in open woods; where they will be sheltered by an angle of the house or a slope of ground; or on hillsides protected from prevailing winds.

In setting out evergreens, the greatest care should be taken not to disturb the roots; it is not necessary to remove the burlap; turn it down from around the top before planting is finished, and make several long cuts with a knife if the burlap is extra heavy; plenty of peat moss in the soil will help supply the moisture necessary for the tops while the roots are becoming established in their new quarters.

As practically all of the broadleaved evergreens are included in the ericaceous plants (see page 11) and prefer a somewhat acid-reacting soil, peat moss suits them ideally. One of the largest specialists in rhododendrons, laurel, azaleas, and similar plants uses granulated peat moss by the carload, employing it in all his planting and transplanting, although he is located in the Pennsylvania mountains in the heart of the rhododendron district, where natural "kalmia soil" is available in an quantity. A leading landscape architect in Massachusetts has made the statement that he saved a large planting of rhododendron, laurel, and azaleas by the use of peat moss after the plants were almost given up. In many commercial establishments specializing in the propagation of the broadleaved evergreens, such as the Koster Nursery mentioned on page 2, peat moss is found to be absolutely essential in their work.

Mulching. The remarks made above concerning the mulching of evergreens apply with equal force to the broadleaved evergreens. Once they become well established, they protect and shade the soil beneath their spreading branches; but until that time, a mulch of peat moss will serve as a most grateful substitute for the layer of moisture retaining and acid reacting humus which would cover their roots under natural conditions. Strawey manure, sometimes employed for this purpose, should never be used, because it tends to neutralize the acid condition of the soil, and thus check growth. With plenty of peat moss in the soil and on top of it, there is no place, providing climatic conditions are suitable, where the broad-leaved evergreens may not be grown.

I wonder if the sap is stirring yet,
If wintry birds are dreaming of a mate,
If frozen snowdrops feel as yet the sun
And crocus fires are kindling one by one:
Sing, robin, sing:
I still am sore in doubt concerning spring.

—C. ROSSETTI

The spring flowering bulbs are the glory of the early garden—but the critical period in their culture comes *after* they have bloomed. Hardy lilies, such as auratum (insert), like their roots kept cool and moist during mid-summer. Peat moss helps with both.

CHAPTER VIII

MAKING SURE OF RESULTS WITH LILIES
AND BULBS

Next to the rose in historic interest, in literature, and in universal appeal, comes the lily. Its stately beauty and graceful charm, no less than all the wealth of association which surrounds it like an aura, make the lily a welcome guest in any garden. And yet, in the majority of gardens, one may look for lilies in vain.

The reason? Partly because there are real difficulties in the way of growing them which sometimes cause failure, but more because of the imagined difficulties which prevent many beginners from trying them at at all. Culturally, the lilies have a poor reputation, much poorer than they actually deserve. It is not so much that they are difficult in their cultural requirements, but *different,* which has caused most of the trouble.

For the lilies, like the evergreens, are denizens of mountains, valleys and meadows, and not really creatures of man-made gardens. Most of those in cultivation are the original species. Often thriving wonderfully in what would seem to be most unpromising situations in the wilds, they do poorly when we try to bring them to the luxury and shelter of our protected garden closes. The best rules to follow in growing lilies, as with evergreens, is to try to reproduce as far as feasible, *the conditions under which they naturally grow.* Of these, more later.

Most of the other bulbous flowers, however, are among the easiest of all plants to grow. Even the wholly inexperieneced beginner may confidently expect success with such things as the "Dutch" bulbs—tulips, daffodils, crocuses, and so forth—or with gladiolus and cannas, at his very first attempt with them. This is largely because the grower of the bulb has done most of the work for him. The bulbs themselves contain enough stored up plant food to give good results—*for the first season;* to continue to get good results, however, is "something else

55

again:" often the bulbs "run out" rapidly. Some suggestions concerning what to do to prevent this are given later in this chapter.

The Three Big Essentials With Hardy Lilies

A number of the hardy lilies, and some of the most beautiful ones, are native over a large part of the United States. If you have ever roamed the woods or fields, you have undoubtedly come across specimens of the yellow meadow lily (L. canadense), the red wood lily (L. philadelphicum) or the orange-red, brown spotted "Turks-cap" (L. superbum) which is one of the most magnificent of all lilies. Last August I found a spot where these grew over nine feet tall, some with over two dozen flowers and buds on each stalk. What a thrill a plant explorer would have gotten to have discovered them in some untravelled and inacessible region; but here, where with a little effort they may be searched out within a few miles of almost any town, or even city, they are given little more consideration than weeds; no wonder they resent it when we attempt to bring them into captivity!

Whether you go lily hunting on your own account, or are content to sit at home and read the thrilling adventures of such men as E. H. Wilson, who brought the wonderful Regal Lily from the wilds of Thibet, you will note that the hardy lilies almost without exception are discovered in a habitat which supplies, first of all, excellent drainage, so that there is no standing water about the bulb, even though it may be growing in a low, moist place; second, a peaty or an acid soil usually, though sometimes one of a calcerous, stoney character; and lastly, a soil the surface of which is covered with plant growth, such as the meadow grasses in the case of the meadow lily, or with a mulch of natural humus, as in the case of the wood lily. Bare soil and the hardy lilies are not found together.

Good Drainage. What has already been said concerning drainage for roses (see page 43) applies almost without amendment to lilies. In most garden soils no artificial drainage need be put in. If the soil itself is naturally inclined to be somewhat heavy and to stay wet, it will be greatly benefitted by the addition of coal ashes, as already suggested. It may be possible that the ashes contain too much lime to suit some varieties.

I have never noticed this in my own experience, but I have not tried them all and am not prepared to say. My own experience has been extensive enough, however, to convince me that there has been a lot of nonsense written about lime and lilies. I am certain that many varieties for which either an acid soil or a lime soil are prescribed as an absolute necessity, are fairly "tolerant" of soils which show a slight reaction in the opposite direction. Personally I think there is no doubt that many of the results, both favorable and unfavorable, which have been ascribed to acid-reacting or to lime soils, have been due to other causes.

I have grown many varieties of lilies successfully in soil in which both ashes and leaf mould (usually more acid in its reaction than granulated peat moss) were freely used. I believe that an abundance of available moisture, *without* any *danger of standing water,* is much more important to most varieties than an extreme in either lime or acid soil condition. Provision may be made for supplying abundant moisture without standing water by using plenty of ashes and plenty of peat moss in the preparation of the lily bed. For those lilies which seem to prefer a distinctly lime soil, ground limestone may be added when the bed is made.

Fertilizers and Manures. One of the biggest dangers in growing lilies is that the bulbs will fail to get a good start. Before the root system is established they are particularly subject to injury, from rotting in wet soil, fungus diseases or the destruction of the leaf scales from contact with manure or chemical fertilizer. No stable manure excepting that which is so decayed as to have become humus rather than manure, and no chemical fertilizers, should be used. Even such comparatively safe fertilizers as bone meal and wood ashes should be employed with care. My own preference in fertilizer to be used with lilies are fine and coarse bone, a small amount of tankage, wood ashes and tobacco fertilizer—omitting the wood ashes for acid-loving varieties. These are mixed thoroughly through the soil, and never placed immediately around the bulb.

Planting. Some lilies form roots on the stem above the bulb, and others only from the base of the bulb. The former are known as "stem-rooting" and the latter as "base-rooting" lilies. The stem-rooting sorts should be planted much deeper. The best catalogs give the necessary information as to the proper planting of each variety, as these vary greatly—from a few inches to a foot in depth. Dig a hole which will take the bulb easily without any crowding, as the scales are easily broken off; place several inches of sand in the bottom of the hole, if the soil is at all heavy, in which to set the bulb. I like to mix an extra handful or two of peat moss in the soil before putting in the sand, so that the growing roots may be sure to find plenty of moisture when they are ready for it. (See illustration on page 48.) As a safeguard, dust the bulbs thoroughly with Semesan before planting.

Mulching. Most hardy lily bulbs are planted in the soil as soon as they are received from the seedsman, which is often quite late. An effectual winter mulch is therefore doubly important; it delays the freezing of the soil to the depth of the bulb, allowing more time for root development, as well as keeping the surface in better condition through the winter and spring.

The importance of a summer mulch for bulbs has already been made plain. There is no material better for this purpose than granulated peat moss—and incidently none which gives a neater, better appearance to the garden.

Getting Better Results With Bulbs

Speaking culturally, rather than botanically, the flowering bulbs may be considered in two main groups; those which bloom in the spring, and those which flower during summer and autumn.

The spring-flowering bulbs almost always bloom satisfactorily the first spring after being planted, for reasons already explained, and also because, during the winter and spring, there is quite certain to be an abundance of moisture in the soil. But—and a very important "but" it is—the following season's results depend upon the growth made by the plant *after the flowers have bloomed and gone.* The foliage of tulips and daffodils, for instance, is not fully matured and ripened until late in June, unless dry soil and other adverse conditions cause it to die prematurely, in which event, the flowers for the following year will suffer.

GROWING BULBS INDOORS

Forcing in water

Forcing in fibre

Growing in pot

FORCING BULBS IN FIBRE

Cover to tips of bulbs

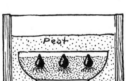

Place in dark to make roots

Bring into cool temperature

Higher temperature full sunlight

FORCING IN SOIL

Bulbs in bulb pan

Bringing into heat

Cross section of pot

Burying out of doors for root growth

Paper cone over Hyacinth to draw up Spike

From The Book of Bulbs—*Rockwell.* Courtesy Macmillan Company.

It is, therefore, quite as important to prepare thoroughly the soil for these bulbs so that there will be moisture and plant food in abundance in the soil, as it is for other flowers. In Holland, where the various spring-flowering bulbs have been produced commercially for so many generations, moisture is always available a few inches below the surface, being supplied by the innumerable canals which form a net work through the bulb fields. Of course, it is not feasible to have a little canal in your own home garden, but a generous amount of peat moss in the soil, to store away the surplus water from the spring rains until the bulbs need it when hot dry weather arrives, is the next best thing to that. Bulb roots revel in the moist humus of decaying peat moss. I have used it in planting bulbs under most adverse conditions, always with extremely satisfactory results. There is no danger of getting too much of it; the more the better.

Summer-Blooming Bulbs. For bulbs blooming in summer and autumn, which make their maximum growth during the driest season in the year, peat moss in the soil, well beneath the surface, is helpful for obvious reasons. *It is particularly important for bulbs planted where the surface soil cannot readily be cultivated.* Here peat moss as a mulch on top of the soil, as well as in the soil, will produce results such as cannot be secured without it.

Winter Storing of Bulbs. If you have dahlia bulbs, tuberous rooted begonias, gladiolus corms, or anything similar to keep through the winter, peat moss makes an ideal medium in which to safely store them. Due to its exceptional insulating properties it preserves the natural moisture within the tubers or bulbs, alike preventing shriveling, and avoiding excessive moisture, which causes decay. Many years ago, I hit upon the idea of using sphagnum moss for the winter storing of roots and bulbs. I described this in one of my books, and thought I had made a great "find;" but granulated peat moss has proved so much better that I now use it exclusively for this purpose. If you have had trouble in keeping your dahlia tubers, try this method and I am sure you will experience the same happy results.

First April, She with mellow showers
Opens the way to early flowers;
Then after her comes smiling May
In a more rich and sweet array;
Next enters June, and brings us more
Gems than these two that went before:
Then lastly July comes, and she
More wealth brings in than all those three!

—HERRICK

A hardy border like this? What a place to work in, to play in, to loaf in! And, you can have one! Many of the flowers are easily grown from seed; others you can readily propagate from plants. Why not?

CHAPTER IX

HARDY PERENNIALS AND ROCK PLANTS

The hardy perennials, since "Grandmother's hardy garden" has returned to popular favor, have been used more generally than any other type of plants. The fact that they succeed over a wide variation of soil, and in many extremes of climate, is self evident.

A fairly heavy garden loam, with good "body," is supposed to be best for the general run of hardy perennials. We are told, however, that they may be grown in lighter soil by the use of heavy applications of well-decayed barnyard manure. As a matter of fact, I have grown a very representative list of hardy perennials, in the lighest of light sandy soil, without any manure whatsoever.

There is nothing miraculous about barnyard manure or the results obtained with it. It supplies to the soil a large quantity of moisture retaining humus, and some of the essential plant foods, particularly nitrogen, in immediately available form. If we supply the humus and the available plant foods in other materials, we can get results comparable to those obtained with manure. Peat moss will supply the former, and for the latter there are a number of fertilizers. Most of the perennials are not at all sensitive concerning the forms in which plant foods are served them. All of the organic or animal fertilizers, such as bone, tankage and dried blood, and the vegetable fertilizers, like cotton seed meal and tobacco may be used liberally without any danger of injury. Even chemicals and chemical fertilizers may be utilized if applied with care; but personally, I always prefer to stick to the others, which I consider not only safer but better.

Dividing and Replanting. Many perennials under favorable conditions make so vigorous a growth that at the end of the second or third year, the clumps or crowns have become overcrowded with shoots, and must be separated into smaller pieces and replanted if we want them to continue to give us the best flowers of which they are capable. This work may be done in either late autumn, when the foliage has died down, or in early spring, before the new growth has started to any extent.

I have found peat moss particularly useful for mixing with the soil when replanting, both because it helps to secure quick, vigorous root-action, and because there is less danger of the soil, after heavy rain, settling away from the newly planted clumps.

Perennials From Seed. Not only because it is more economical, but also because it is more fun, the home gardener will find it worth while to start many of his perennial plants from seed. The money so saved will then be available for purchasing plants of some of the fine new things the seed of which is not yet available, or such others as do not come true from seed, and must be purchased in plant form.

In chapter III, raising plants from seed is discussed in some detail. For the last few years, in starting perennials I have used peat moss not only in the seed bed, but when transplanting the seedlings into a frame. The result has been such root systems as I never before obtained. Many of them, when ready for the second transplanting, lift with such masses of fiberous roots and peat moss soil, that they look wholly out of porportion to the tops, and have to be trimmed down considerably for convenience in handling and planting.

Mulching. Winter mulching is usually recommended for perennials, particularly for the first season after planting, and it is of course necessary every winter for many of the less hardy and half hardy varieties. For the latter, peat moss may be applied more thickly than ordinary mulching materials, because it is light in weight and will not pack down; the plants being mulched are in no danger of being either crushed or suffiocated. Another great advantage of peat moss for all mulching purposes, and particularly for the perennial border, is that it *brings no weed seeds.*

Rock Plants

With each passing season, rock plants are becoming more popular. Even the general catalogs which, a few years ago, contained no mention of rock gardens, now carry special lists of rock garden plants, or use some special method of indicating the sorts which may be employed in rock garden planting.

Many of our well known low-growing annuals and perennials are suitable for rock gardens. These, of course, require no special conditions or treatment. Many of the true rock plants, and especially the alpines, however, will not succeed under general garden conditions. In nature, they are found where an unusual combination of circumstances give them a dry or perfectly drained surface on which the tops may grow, excellent drainage about the main mass of roots, and yet constant moisture lower down, within reach of the unusually long roots which go out after it. Some of them grow in a chalk formation with a high lime content, and others only where the soil reaction is decidedly acid.

Soil which contains a large percentage of peat moss, because of its open porous character, dries off quickly on the surface after a rain or watering, and yet, as we know, holds abundant moisture in reserve beneath the surface. In these two respects, then, it is admirably adapted to rock plants. A soil made up of one part each of good garden loam, peat moss, and sharp sand, will suit the majority of these plants. Stone chips or gravel may be added. Anything approaching clay should be carefully avoided, even in the mixture. For those varieties which are most particular about having an absolutely dry surface on which to rest, such as the thick, woolly-leaved alpines, stone chips may be spread on top of the soil. Pebbles are sometimes used, and answer the purpose so far as the plants are concerned, but they look out of place in a rock garden. Plants which are known to require lime may be placed in pockets filled with soil to which lime has been added. Or one corner of the rock garden may be filled with lime soil and reserved for this class of plants.

I have had occasion to make so many claims for the merits of granulated peat moss in the course of the various types of plants which we have discussed so far, that I almost hesitate to add here the following letter from a very prominent nurseryman who has specialized in ground plants and native plants, often used for the semi-wild rock garden. So far as my own experience has gone, however, in growing this type of plants, it bears out the following:

"Three years ago I put in a wild garden in a hurry very late in the fall. Being extremely familiar with wild garden work and the character of soils required by the various wild plants to be used, I was in a quandary, as I could not at that time obtain the necessary leaf mould and various other soils suited for this long list of plants, most all of them seeming to require different character of soil; drainage, etc. So I took a chance on using two parts peat moss to one part of soil for the entire wild garden planting, without making any distinction as to whether the plans liked peat moss soil or not.

The results of this particular planting are almost unbelievable. Plants like wintergreen, partridge berry, orchids, trilliums, violas, and hypaticas and at least twenty five other wild plants have flourished amazingly in this preparation!"

Unconscious of a less propitious clime
There blooms exotic beauty, warm and snug
While the winds whistle and the snows descend.

Who does not love the garden that blooms indoors! Even if you do not possess a "sunspot" such as this, there are many plants which will thrive in any sunny window. (Photograph above is by courtesy of Hitchings & Co.)

CHAPTER X

PLANTS IN THE HOUSE

When winter has captured the world out of doors, and our gardens—despite all we may do towards keeping a bit of cheer with evergreens and bright berried plants—are flower and song-forsaken, then how welcome is some green plant blossoming indoors, even though it be but a single geranium in a pot on the window sill!

In Grandmother's day, the hardy garden out of doors almost invariably had its supplement in the tender garden within doors, for the winter months. For a while, both went out of fashion. The hardy garden has come back: this time, undoubtedly to stay. Are we to have a similar reflorescence of the indoor garden?

I think there are not lacking indications that we may. I know that I have received during the last few years an increasing percentage of inquiries concerning house plants, from the readers of the several magazines for which I write, and that also a number of the old favorite indoor flowers are finding their way back into catalogs from which they have long been absent. The ever increasing number of sun parlors—or as they might more correctly be termed, "sun-living-rooms"—in itself constitutes a growing invitation to home owners to have more plants indoors.

House Plants In General

Many persons have tried house plants only to meet with indifferent success, if not actual failure. The reason is usually ascribed to lack of sunlight, or to high temperature or low temperature, too much water or too little water, improper soil, lack of the requisite "knack" with plants, and so on down the line to potting the plants "in the wrong phase of the moon!"

In nine cases out of ten, however, it is none of these things, but merely the fact that in the super-dry atmosphere still to be found in most modern residences, it is practically impossible to keep either the plants themselves, or the soil in the pots in which they grow, from drying out. The thirsty air sucks up any available moisture so quickly that even if the plants are watered regularly, there are such extremes of dry and wet that their growth will be severely interfered with. There is no *constancy* of soil moisture (see page 14).

What House Plants Need. It would take several chapters the size of this to cover even briefly all the details of growing plants indoors. But I can tell you in a few sentences—almost in a few words—the two elementary requisites for success. With these provided, almost anyone can grow house plants: without them, no matter how much fussing and care may be bestowed, success is not possible.

The first of these two things is to get the air back to a normal moisture content. (You should do this anyway, whether you expect to grow plants or not, because air with the moisture driven out of it is one of the most prolific sources of the various "winter" diseases of humans, particularly those attacking the throat.) The remedy is easy: merely provide the air with plenty of water to drink. There are now available evaporators, in the form of very deep, narrow tanks, designed to hang on the ordinary radiator, and being concealed at the back. For hot air furnaces, there is a device which *automatically* keeps the water-pan, supplied with the furnace, filled with water. Even without the assistance of such devices, it is a simple matter to keep an attractive flower bowl, or some similar container, on or near the radiator in each room; or to make yourself acquire the habit of filling the furnace water pan regularly, once a day, instead of using it merely to hold coal dust and ashes.

The second essential is to provide a soil suitable for the plants which are grownig in pots. Most garden soils, even though they may produce splendid flowers out of doors, are not fit for plants in pots. A potted plant has only a fraction of the root-pasturage which is available to one growing in the open. A soil for potting, in which the great majority of plants you are likely to try will grow vigorously, is easily mixed as follows:

One part top soil, or good garden loam, (not clay).

One part manure, preferably cow manure, old enough to be fine and crumbly.

One part peat moss.

To this mixture, if the soil used is at all heavy, some sand, —5 to 10%—may be added. Mix through it also fine bone, 1 to 2 pints to the bushel. If decomposed manure is not available, use half soil and half peat moss, adding shredded cow manure, stable manure, or sheep manure, any of which may be obtained from almost any seed dealer or florist.

General Care. With these two essentials provided for, it is not difficult to succeed with the fairly extensive list of plants which may be grown under ordinary house conditions, where the night temperature does not go much below 45°. Where there is plenty of sunshine, quite a number of flowering plants will do nicely. Ferns and several of the decorative foliage plants may be grown where there is not sunshine enough to suit the flowering sorts.

Ferns, because of their many desirable qualities, and the fact that they will thrive in partial shade, are the most popular of all plants for the house. For the growth of ferns, peat moss gives wonderful results. The change which sickly appearing ferns undergo in a month's time when placed in a mixture of half soil and half peat moss is almost unbelievable. Here again the water holding capacity of peat moss becomes of particular importance since the dry atmosphere of a heated house causes high evaporation from the mass of fern foliage. Then too, the peat moss seems to have just the right nutrient materials for ferns.

Watering house plants is always one of the biggest problems. They require much more moisture when they are in active growth than during the "rest periods" which almost all plants undergo at some season of the year. During the short days of winter, even those plants which are in an active state of growth will require very much less water than later in the spring, as the days get warmer and longer. The use of plenty of peat moss in the potting soil greatly simplifies the problem of wat·ering, as such a soil will not get wet and soggy even if more water than necessary is given—assuming of course that drainage is provided for, by placing pieces of broken pots, a few small cinders, or some similar material in the bottoms of pots larger than four inches in diameter. This winter, by using a peat moss compost, I have grown a number of plants satisfactorily without any surface watering at all; the pots are kept in pans or shallow bowls in which about half an inch of water is maintained; the plants seem to take what they require, and so far, all have done well. This is much less trouble than watering them in the ordinary way.

We have seen that the wilting, or even dying off, of house plants is due to the extreme dryness of the atmosphere, more than to any other one cause. I have used moistened granulated peat moss to fill in around a pot in a jardiniere. Seemingly, sufficient moisture is drawn through the porous pot by capillary action to supply the potted plant with all the moisture it needs. This also prevents water collecting at the bast of the pot, and thus improves the drainage. Furthermore, the air about the plants will also be kept somewhat moist and cool, a condition favoring healthy growth.

Plant Food

Plants making vigorous growth are likely to soon exhaust one or more of the plant food elements in the limited amount of soil they must be grown in. One of the many highly concentrated but evenly balanced house plant foods may be used to maintain strong growth and the production of flowers. These are readily obtainable from seed stores and florists.

Forcing Bulbs In Peat Moss

One of the most entertaining, satisfactory and easiest methods of having an abundance of flowers in the house during the winter months is to grow bulbs. They may be put either in clay pots or bulb pans, or in the beautifully colored attractive bulb bowls (see page 59) which are now so plentiful and reasonable in price.

Bulbs In Peat Moss Fibre

Most seed stores now sell both the prepared peat moss bulb fibre, and pure peat moss, for the forcing of bulbs. These materials have rapidly replaced the practice of growing them in pebbles and water, both because the results are more satisfactory, and because practically all bulbs may be grown by this method, whereas the varieties suitable for growing in pebbles or water are limited. When granulated peat moss, or peat moss bulb fibre, is used, the bulbs may be grown in bulb bowls without any drainage holes, thus eliminating the danger of having dirty drainage water soil table covers or furniture finish. Thoroughly saturate the peat moss, allowing surplus moisture to drain off. Then fill the bowls nearly full and bury the bulbs up to their necks.

The peat moss or fibre will absorb and hold sufficient moisture to enable the bulbs to get their preliminary root development without further watering. The following directions are quoted from the author's "Book of Bulbs."

"Bulbs which are planted in fibre (or peat moss) may be put in a closet or in a cellar to develop roots, but it is far better to put them out of doors where they can be completely buried, and be brought in as needed. The advantages of doing this, instead of merely putting them in a closet or cellar, are several. In the first place, they can all be *planted at one time,* instead of making several different plantings in succession, as will be necessary to obtain a succession of blooms, if they are kept indoors. In the second place, the conditions under which the roots are produced will much more nearly approximate the natural growth of the bulbs out doors, resulting in a maximum development of the root system, with a minimum growth of tops. And in the third place, the weight of the covering material over them will hold them in position, instead of allowing them to be forced up by the growth of the roots, as sometimes happens when they are merely kept in the dark without any covering over them. Where it is not convenient to provide as many bowls or jardinieres as may be required to plant a quantity to store them in this way, they may be planted in bulb pans, which will fit into the containers in which one may wish to have them flower in the house.

Preliminary Root Development. After planting, the first object is to develop root growth, while holding the top growth in check. If no space outdoors is available, place the bowls, pans or pots in the cellar or in a cool, well ventilated closet, away from the light; have them as completely in the dark as possible; the longer they can be kept here without top growth starting the better. When they are two or three inches high, and the fibre is fairly well filled with roots, remove them to a cool room, and keep out of direct sunlight until the tops, which will be somewhat white and "drawn," show green and more vigorous growth. Water them very moderately at first, but keep the fibre evenly saturated. Care is required in this respect as it may *look* moist even when fairly well dried out. If too much is added at a time, the surplus may be drained from bowls, pans or pots by tilting them up on edge, meanwhile holding the contents in place with the fingers.

As the buds begin to develop, bring the plants into full light, preferably where they will receive direct sunlight at least part of the day, and where the temperature is higher, but be sure that they get plenty of fresh air.

After the plants come into bloom, the flowers will last much longer if they can be kept in a somewhat cooler temperature, particularly during the night.

While a closet or cellar will serve as a place in which to develop the roots, if no outside space is available, it is much better, as has been suggested, to bury the containers outside. Plunge the pots up to the rims in cinders or soil, and cover with 6 inches or more of leaf mould or peat moss. Even in the cellar, it is of advantage to cover the containers with three or four inches of peat moss during the storage period."

The following quotation is interesting as indicating how perfectly adapted peat moss is to the forcing of flower bulbs; it is taken from the Florists' Exchange, (one of the trade papers of the commercial florists,) and it describes a prize winning exhibit of bulbs grown in England:

"Just what may be done with bulbs in fiber is indicated in the accompanying illustration. This remarkable exhibit was staged at the early March Royal Horticultural Society's meeting, by R. H. Bath, Ltd. of Wisbeck, one of the largest bulb growing firms in England. For some years this firm has made a practice of staging, at several successive spring meetings, collections of bulbs grown in fiber, and it is conceeded by everyone, including the best Holland growers, that Bath's are unapproachable in the art of growing bulbs without soil. The group shown was awarded the R .H. S. gold medal, the highest award ever given to such an exhibit; this award has rarely been given to exhibits grown in the ordinary way. . . . In the United States this business of growing in fiber has only been scratched on the surface."

There are some bulbs such as Paper White narcissus, the Chinese Sacred lily, the lily-of-the-valley, freesias, and oxalis, which may be grown with little or no preliminary root development. It is best, however, to keep them in a cool dark place for ten days to two weeks after planting to keep the tops from coming along too rapidly while the roots are getting a start.

FINIS

And so here comes to a close this little volume on gardening with peat moss. The various subjects covered have not been treated in full detail, for the very obvious reason that limited space has made it necessary to confine the discussion to those phases of growing in which the use of peat moss is directly or indirectly concerned. The use of granulated peat moss in horticulture is comparatively new. In this first attempt to present the subject to the American garden public, the authors fully realize both the limitations of their own experience and the fact that much yet remains to be discovered in practical work and by scientific research. They trust, however, that what they have had to say may stimulate a greater interest in what promises to be one of the most helpful materials yet discovered for both commercial and amateur gardening.